Donated By

The

Shamrock Foods Company

The

Shamrock

Way

A legacy to share:

The

Treating employees like family

Shamrock

and customers like friends.

Way

by Mervyn Kaufman

foreword by Barry M. Goldwater

Arizona Historical Foundation
Hayden Library • Arizona State University
Tempe, Arizona 85287-1006

Library of Congress Catalog Card Number:
96-86425

ISBN: 0-910152-16-0

The Shamrock Way
A legacy to share: Treating employees
like family and customers like friends.

Published by Arizona Historical Foundation
Tempe, Arizona
U.S.A.

Printed in the U.S.A.

10 9 8 7 6 5 4 3 2 1

Contents

Illustrations

Foreword

The Shamrock story is a tale of many parts. For spirited capitalists, it is a celebration of the free enterprise system and the rewards explicit in hard work, self-sacrifice, and individual initiative. Those interested in history will find the narrative a stirring testament to the economic vigor and determination that made the United States a powerful nation and the West a proud and productive region. At its heart, it is the saga of a dynamic family—the McClellands—and the contributions three generations have made to both the economy of Arizona and the quality of life enjoyed by its residents.

W. T. McClelland set the stage for the odyssey when he immigrated to the United States from Ireland in 1912 and ten years later established the Shamrock Dairy in Tucson with the help of his wife, "Winnie." At that time, the old pueblo was a bustling settlement connected to the outside world by a fairly sophisticated rail and communication network. The list of businesses and services was expanding annually, as was the population. This was primarily a result of large-scale Eastern investment in mining and ranching, the emergence of the resort industry, and a steady queue of health seekers in pursuit of a desert cure for their various ailments.

Commercial dairies, wedded as they were to developments in irrigation, were almost exclusively limited to the irrigated valleys. The industry as a whole had received a positive boost in the 1890s, when ranchers began to grow alfalfa as a year-round food source for cattle. In the 1920s, competition was fierce, and the market for milk and milk products was fickle. Maricopa County boasted more than half a dozen dairies, for example. Although Flagstaff had only one dairy, Pima County claimed nine, including the McClellands' operation along the banks of the Rillito River.

With so many competitors in the field and a statewide population of less than half a million, the dairy business in the 1920s was not one suited to the timid. Add the cyclical nature of agricultural economics since the industrial age, and even the most casual observer can easily discern why most of

Arizona's early dairies changed hands multiple times or simply ceased activities entirely within the first few years of operation.

In subsequent pages, readers will be treated to a story of a pioneer family of Arizonans who proved the exception to the rule. From grandfather to grandson, the McClellands have systematically built a reputation for quality products, superb customer service, equitable labor practices, and community service few families can match.

They have helped raise Arizona to twenty-first place in the nation in the production of milk and milk products, and at the same time they have become the ninth largest food-service distributor in the United States, serving customers in Arizona, New Mexico, Texas, Nevada, Colorado, Wyoming, Utah, Nebraska, Kansas, and southern California. They have made products bearing the Shamrock logo a commonplace feature in Southwestern households and businesses for nearly three-quarters of a century. Considering the transitory nature of the setting and the inherent instability of the dairy and food-service industries, their growth seems as much a feat as it is an historic fact.

BARRY M. GOLDWATER
SCOTTSDALE, AZ
MARCH 1996

Preface

The past fifty years represent a period of amazing economic growth for our country. In the decades following World War II, the United States as a whole enjoyed a tremendous competitive advantage over other nations. American factories and business techniques led the world, and peoples from the far reaches of the globe beat a path to our door, to learn from us and to adapt. Our economy fueled the expansion of the postwar era and provided the impetus for us to lead the world successfully in the struggle to contain and ultimately defeat militant communism.

Here in Arizona the growth we experienced was nothing short of phenomenal. Our farms grew in number, our industries blossomed, our population soared, and great cities such as Phoenix and Tucson emerged. My father had come from Ireland to an Arizona that had just achieved statehood but was still largely a somnolent frontier. But it's a sleepy little corner of the world no longer. In Arizona today, high-tech manufacturing and a growing service sector are setting the pace. And looking ahead to the twenty-first century, we see a business climate that promises to be vastly different from what we have experienced in the preceding five decades, and a far cry from what Dad found when he settled here and began dairy farming.

The new economic frontier has shifted beyond our state and national borders to Eastern Europe, to Russia, Ukraine, and China. Aggressive competitors are now gathering strength in Japan, Korea, and a unified Germany. For Arizonans, as for all Americans, it is no longer enough to do as we have done in the past. We must work harder and more creatively just to hold on to what we have. If we wish to grow and prosper, then as citizens we must commit ourselves to world-class performance in every field.

For all of us at Shamrock Foods Company, such performance has resulted in our being number one—in the quality of what we produce, in the gross profits we register, and ultimately in our share of the market. By the mid-1990s, we had become an $800 million company with a comprehensive growth plan designed to push us toward the $1 billion mark by the year 2000. We have never felt complacent; if anything, we have been *driven*—and when I say "we," I refer not just to myself and my immediate family but also to a finely honed team of executives and managers at the division level plus staff members at every level and in each location. It is for this sterling group, the dedicated people who have been the spine and sinew of our company, that this book is written—people who, in many instances, were pioneers like my parents, people who followed afterward and invested their energy in helping us expand, and people who in the future will make their way in life by being part of our company. All will find that the history of Shamrock Foods parallels the history of the region, that the Shamrock spirit that infuses our company is reflected in Arizona's own remarkable growth.

I think a great many people have grown considerably by being part of Shamrock. I can see it in myself, certainly, and in my sister, Frances, over the years. I remember, long ago, her coming to talk to me and asking, "Norman, why do you want this company to be any bigger?" My response, as I remember it, was that "we have no choice. It has to grow or it will stagnate." I am not sure that answer satisfied her completely, but I think she came to understand in time.

Frances and I had both been through business school. We understood that even in the most successful enterprise, expenses invariably grow over time as a result of inflation and other uncontrollable factors. And we learned that the way to deal with rising expenses was not simply to allow the cost of goods to rise and then, to compensate, raise prices. From my earliest association with Shamrock, I felt it was important to push our costs down. I was convinced that doing this would make our customers want to use *our* product in preference to that of our competitors and that they could afford to buy more of it. And it was reasonable to assume that the more product we sold, the greater our market share would be. So we resolved to enable our customers to buy less expensively, as long as there was no sacrifice of quality. The longer we were in business, the more we realized that if we did not have a quality product, our reputation would suffer, our volume would shrink, and our cost of processing and distributing would soar. That is one reason quality has always been central at Shamrock.

Studying economics, you learn that the more you lower your price, the more product you can sell. So we knew that the lower our costs, the better off we would be vis-`a-vis our competition. That is why, like my father, I have always been keen to be number one—the dominant player—in our market. Being the biggest doesn't necessarily make you the least costly, but you *can* be if you do it right—if you let your market share help you drive your prices. A company like Shamrock can never *save* itself into making a profit. We have been able to contain unit cost not only by increasing volume but also by developing systems that enable us to function, and deliver, more efficiently.

New technology has helped substantially, but what has really propelled us into the forefront has been our ability to attract talented, dedicated people who share our Shamrock values. I am proud of the people we have and of the growth we have been able to achieve together, at times under extremely difficult conditions— initially, against a phalanx of major competitors across this state. Not only have we survived, but in the dairy operation, the foundation of our company, we have landed squarely on top. We are not just coasting either. Our people are out there every month, every week, every day, making new promotional arrangements for our products and responding to the needs of our customers. And our thinking extends well beyond day-to-day challenges and concerns.

One of the responsibilities an owner or leader has is keeping the future in focus. You have to determine where you want a company to go, long term, and where you hope it will be in the next year or even two, three, or four years down the road. I believe that in a successful organization of any kind there must be somebody who can point out periodically the direction that should be taken and what should be accomplished along the way. Even in the midst of a firefight, I have done that kind of thinking, and I imagine that for the foreseeable future I will continue to be the person who makes the final call, just as my father did even when I had begun running the show.

I consider myself decisive; I think, too, that I am probably driven. And if I have either of these traits, it is undoubtedly due to my father. He was a man who dealt head-on with tough problems, with the gritty issues that many companies unwisely try to sweep under the rug. From him I learned that if you don't confront the issues, things start to slip, and soon you are avoiding rather than eliminating the big stumbling blocks. I was trained not to do that; it was not the Shamrock way.

My parents had high expectations of their children, of both Frances and me. They expected us to be motivated to succeed. They had come to this country with little except determination and were extremely proud of what they had accomplished, though they tended to be humble about it. Dad had only an eighth-grade education and was always a little embarrassed that, unlike Mother, he was not a college graduate. Intellectually, he was never as sure of himself as she, but he was every bit as positive and single minded. His strong suits were common sense and an enormous capacity for work.

Once he got an idea in his head that a particular plan of action would succeed, he strived to make sure it did. He loved to think long term, and his thinking was always sound. People had confidence in him, not only our employees but our customers as well. Whatever he said he would do, he did. That gave people a feeling of security. Today, although Shamrock has expanded beyond the Arizona borders—into Texas, New Mexico, Kansas, Nebraska, Nevada, Utah, Wyoming, Colorado, and California—the culture of the company remains as Dad and Mother instinctively defined it: honesty and integrity are paramount; success is predicated on our ability to treat employees like family and customers like friends.

When I was a high school student, I was sure I would never go into business with my father, but when I finally did, I found Dad to be the easiest person in the world to be in business with. He let me do whatever I wanted and held me accountable for all of it, which I always considered a wise approach. Now, as Shamrock's chairman, I am trying to follow a similar course with my son, Kent, who, as president, is responsible for operations. We have a very close association—closer, I think, that I had with my father. It's something I have worked hard to achieve.

I was pleased when Kent joined the Young Presidents' Organization a few years ago. I had joined it, too, before turning forty, and found it enormously helpful. Through that organization, I met a great many gifted people from all parts of the country, men and women whom I could consult with, exchange ideas with, and receive encouragement from. It was largely through the Young Presidents' that I developed the incentive to make Shamrock grow. I studied the success stories and the failures; the group proved an excellent forum.

The idea of sharing information was not exclusively mine. One of the things that endeared this country to my father was that there was always someplace to go for information, someone to turn to with questions about agriculture. He was impressed with the land-grant college system and took an active interest in the University of Arizona. There, he had a close relationship with the people involved in dairy husbandry; they were part of the College of Agriculture. For many years, the McClelland family and Shamrock Foods have enjoyed a fine relationship with the business and agriculture colleges of the university. This relationship has taken many forms, from seeking advice on solving specific problems and hiring graduates to establishing scholarships and donating funds to build a great, new facility at the business college.

It is my hope and belief that, because of this state-of-the-art facility, the students passing through the school in the years to come will have even greater opportunities for achievement, success, and innovation than their predecessors.

It is my hope and belief that they will learn there the basic skills needed to expand the economy of this state and of our nation.

It is also my hope and belief that they will find reinforced there the human traits of integrity, ethical behavior, compassion, and mutual respect that are not only keys to success in the business world but to a full and rewarding life as well. Coincidentally, these traits happen to be the cornerstones of our company's success, the foundation of what we call the Shamrock way.

NORMAN P. MCCLELLAND
PHOENIX, AZ
MARCH 1996

Chapter One

Passing the Torch

*T*he year 1968 was pivotal for Shamrock, a landmark in a singular new era. It was forty-six years after the company's dairy operation began in Tucson, Arizona, two years since the food-service division was established, and one year since Shamrock's three main companies—Shamrock Dairy, Inc., of Tucson; Shamrock Dairy of Phoenix; and Shamrock Milk Transport Company—were merged into a single entity: Shamrock Foods Company.

The year's best news was that the company did $22 million in total sales, a record then. The worst and saddest news surrounded the death, in April, of its chairman and cofounder, W. T. McClelland.

The elder McClelland, known widely as Mr. Mac, had been chairman since 1954, when his son, Norman, became president. Now the chairmanship would pass to Mr. Mac's brother-in-law, William J. Parker. According to Frances McClelland, Mr. Mac's daughter and the company's longtime secretary-treasurer, "Dad was in a car accident in 1960. He wasn't injured, but his blood pressure dropped, and as his doctors could never restore circulation in one leg, it had to be amputated. He never really adjusted to that too well, or to the prosthesis. He experienced continual pain—and frustration. He still came to the dairy, but I'm not sure how actively he was managing it. Probably, it was falling more on Norman at that point and on Uncle."[1] "Uncle" was, of course, Bill Parker, who had been a Shamrock partner since 1933.

OLIVER "OLLIE" STALLINGS
*Assistant Secretary of the Shamrock Board of Directors and,
since 1939, the company's consulting accountant*

Mr. Mac was still at the dairy, in an advisory capacity, after the accident. I'd go down there twice a year and do my work right on the premises. Mr. Mac was really proud of his business. The first thing he would do when I arrived was take me around the plant and show me every change that had been made since I was there the last time. He was not only proud but also protective, a very private person. And by that I mean he didn't want anyone from the outside knowing anything more about his affairs than was necessary. He even hated the IRS coming in, because he thought it was none of their business. Those were the very words he used—"none of their business." It was a privacy thing with him. Mrs. Mac was entirely different, a quiet, relatively unassuming person. She acted as office manager for many years—until the business got real big and illness slowed her down.[2]

DERRELL FAIRFIELD
*Senior Vice President and General Manager of the
Dairy Division until retiring in 1994*

Almost until the day he died, Mr. Mac continued to come to work every morning, right after breakfast. He had the corner office at the Tucson dairy but he didn't spend too much time in it, even then. He never did move up to Phoenix. He'd wear his artificial leg and travel around in a battery-operated golf cart. Fred, his driver, would bring him there, and Mr. Mac would get in the golf cart and make the rounds everywhere. As I remember it, he was still very active for some time.

To me, he didn't seem to be an outgoing person, and naturally I was a little nervous to be around him. But to compound things, it seemed that if I tried to just say, "Good morning, Mr. Mac" and walk right by him, he'd say, "Wait a minute. I want to talk to you. Tell me what's happening now in home delivery." And then it seemed the next time I saw him, I'd say, "Let me tell you what's been happening here," and I'd start explaining something to him. Then suddenly he'd say, "Well, we must get busy, we must get busy" and want to move on.

Mr. Mac was fiercely loyal. When he liked you, had confidence in you, and felt you were his friend, there was nothing he wouldn't do for you. However, if he didn't like you — nothing. He wouldn't even talk to you. But he had a knack for hiring good people. He let them run his business and would back them up completely. And in the early days he and Mrs. Mac talked everything over and made all their decisions together.[3]

With his son, Norman, on the scene to manage the company and direct its growth, Mr. Mac could devote more and more of his time to his cattle. "He had all Guernseys," Derrell Fairfield recalled, "and I think he was active in the American Guernsey Cattle Club and the Arizona club as well. When I joined the dairy, it was like a show herd, a registered Guernsey herd. You'd drive into the dairy and all you would see were the lots filled with Guernseys. At that time we had what we called the Hill Farm, about a mile and a half from the Tucson dairy. They milked some Holsteins there, but right at the dairy it was all Guernseys. Their milk is richer. They produce less than Holsteins do, but the Guernseys' less volume is balanced by more butterfat. And in those days people were looking for good, rich milk."[4]

OLLIE STALLINGS

Mr. Mac had a herd of Guernsey cattle that he owned personally, and he'd sell the milk to the company. He gradually converted to a registered herd in a desire to build up as good a herd as he possibly could during his lifetime. A grade-A herd is a group of animals without pedigrees; a registered herd has pedigreed cattle. Mr. Mac would buy pedigreed Guernseys from time to time, those that had a good background and a history of being top milk producers and good calf producers. He did it to upgrade his herd, and that was as much his life at that point as the dairy had been before. Maybe more so, in a way, because he really loved those animals. They were all given names—Betsy, Sue, Carlotta— and he knew them all by sight. I remember, one time, talking with Mrs. Mac when I was down there working. Mr. Mac had bought a couple of high-priced animals, so I was kind of inquiring about that. I mean, why would he be spending a lot of money for animals? She asked me not to talk to him about it because I might hurt his feelings—because he felt he didn't have too many years left to improve the herd, and he could speed up the process by bringing in outside animals.[5]

The man who became particularly helpful in selecting the Guernsey cattle and in refining Shamrock's breeding program was Clifford Knight, who capped a forty-year career in the cattle business by signing on as a consultant to Shamrock in the 1960s. His primary job was to help Mr. Mac improve the Guernsey herd, a task begun informally when the two men first met, in the '50s.

CLIFFORD "CLIFF" KNIGHT
Longtime family friend and dairy cattle consultant

I didn't get along with him very well at first. For one thing, I didn't have time. I had 4,500 head of dairy cattle and 2,000 acres of farmland to look after. But after a lot of phone calls—he even called my brother and asked, "What's the matter with that brother of yours? Can't you get him to come down?"—I finally agreed to pay him a visit.

"What do you think, Cliff?" he asked when I went through the herd. "Mac," I said, "I can tell you one thing: You're on the wrong track." When I told him he'd gone astray in his breeding program, he turned to Mrs. McClelland and said, "Winnie, you knew this all the time." She said, "I didn't want to hurt your feelings, Mac." "Well," he replied, "this man doesn't care whose feelings he hurts; he'll tell anybody the truth." That's when McClelland and I got to be real buddies.[6]

DR. GARY STOTT
Former head of the Dairy Science Department, University of Arizona

Mr. Mac was always trying to help us out. He was particularly helpful with the breeding. If he had a bull he thought exceptionally good, he would offer it; we would exchange bulls. We would help him with new technology and were always exchanging information with him. When I became head of the department, I was responsible for our herd and a little dairy plant we had on campus.

Mr. Mac was very supportive of us. Sometimes we would have too much milk and not enough cream, and the next time it would be too much cream. Shamrock always helped us out. Everyone trusted Mr. Mac. He did a tremendous job for the dairy industry in this state. When he said that's the way it was, he was right. He had a good reputation. He was a tough-minded businessman, but he would stick to his word. I remember him calling me up and saying, "Gary, come out and talk to me. We're going to talk cows."[7]

In 1968, the W. T. and Winifred McClelland Scholarships were established at the University of Arizona, two $500 scholarships (eventually, four $1,000 scholarships) awarded each year to worthy upperclassmen or graduate students in the College of Agriculture, with preference given to men and women majoring in dairy and food sciences. Years later, Norman and Frances furthered the company's association with the university by funding construction of the new business college known as McClelland Hall, which was dedicated in 1992.

"Although Dad took great pleasure in taking care of the cows in his later years," Norman remembered, "that didn't mean he wasn't there, that he wasn't at the board meetings, that he wasn't chairman of the board, that he was not still in charge of the money."[8] Said David Hall, Shamrock's senior vice president and the man responsible for the company's successful move into food distribution, "I can remember Norman's dad sitting quietly at meetings at a time when we were having price wars that were costing an awful lot of money—we were young kids, Norman and I. Mr. Mac would be pouring coffee for everyone; then after maybe an hour of listening to us not getting anywhere, he might say, 'Have you boys thought of this?' And we would look at each other like dumb bunnies and wonder, 'Why didn't we think of that?' But that would be the extent of it. He didn't say you've got to do this, you've got to do that. He never did."

"You know, a word that's never used at Shamrock is 'boss.' You might say to yourself, 'He's my boss,' but nobody ever says, 'I'm the boss.' You might say, 'I'm in charge of the department,' but you'd never say to somebody, 'I'm your boss.' Norman would never say it, nor would his dad."[9]

Nor would anyone say, "That's not my job," according to Eloise Hayden, whose long career in Accounts Payable began in 1960.

ELOISE HAYDEN
Former accounting clerk in the Phoenix office

If a person was off, we knew enough about each other's work that we could really cover the desk, and if they were sick for a week, why, we'd do their work and our work too. Nobody's job was just their own. Everyone seemed to pitch in and help. Just like playing musical chairs, you'd move from one person's desk to another. The nice thing about working at the Phoenix dairy, especially at the beginning, was the smallness of it. It was nice to walk down the hall and have everybody speak to you and at least know your name. It didn't make any difference what position you had.[10]

Norman recalled that as chairman his father "still had numerous responsibilities, and everyone knew it, including me. He never tried to do your work for you. If you wanted to try something, as far he was concerned you could go ahead and do whatever you wanted, but he expected you to be a cannonball, he expected you to handle things properly, and he expected things to work out the way everyone hoped they would if your plans were successful. Within these guidelines, however, I was pretty much free to do whatever I wished."[11]

FRANCES HELEN McCLELLAND
Secretary-Treasurer of Shamrock Foods Company

My parents were taught not to be frivolous. Each of them grew up believing that everyone had to pull his or her own weight. Everyone, children included, had to work hard to earn a living for the family. And Dad was patriotic. Not long after emigrating from Ireland, he became a citizen, and Mother became a citizen by marrying him. He was very proud of his country; he was very loyal; he voted in every election. Dad was also very generous, feeling that it was important that he give back to the community because it had been kind to him. So he was very good about making contributions to hospitals and churches, and he took advantage of the proximity of the University of Arizona. In exchange, they were able to use our cows and our farm in Tucson for experiments that proved extremely valuable to them—for example, to do something about the breeding problem in the summer when it's really hot. When they came out to the farm, which was only twenty or thirty minutes from the university, they had a ready-made research project to work on.[12]

The early years of Norman's leadership were marked by enormous growth, by numerous acquisitions, and by such additions to the Shamrock menu as ice cream, cottage cheese, and buttermilk, then finally food service and distribution. But perhaps the most crucial and most significant decision made during the first dozen years of his presidency involved entering the Phoenix market. The move was well planned and brilliantly orchestrated; it was also fraught with risk.

OLLIE STALLINGS

I know they felt they had to come up to Phoenix and establish the business here, because if they didn't, they would gradually get squeezed out of the market statewide. There was growth in Tucson, of course, but there was really big growth in Phoenix. I'm sure the McClellands realized that if they went into that market in a really big way and were unsuccessful, they could lose it. So they tried to cut some of the risk by coming in on a modest basis.

At first, they hoped to acquire an existing Phoenix company; it was a co-op they were negotiating to buy because of its routes. That didn't work, but they decided to come on anyway. They just came up here and set up a little distribution base and shipped their products from Tucson for delivery to customers here. But, at first, they didn't have a single customer in Phoenix except my wife and me. So they went out and literally beat the bushes, knocking on doors of every business establishment to get this operation under way.[13]

NORMAN PARKER MCCLELLAND
Chairman of the Board of Shamrock Foods Company

We had to get ourselves in a position where we could strike back at our competition. They were sitting in Phoenix and were able to come down and depress prices in our market, and we were not able to retaliate—because we were only in Tucson, which represented just twenty-five percent of the market. I felt that if we were able to compete successfully with the larger dairy companies in Arizona we would need a plant that enabled us to compete directly with them in the Phoenix market as well as the rest of the state. Otherwise, they could do business at a profit in that part of the state, then undercut us in southern Arizona. Which is exactly what they tried to do. As soon as we came to Phoenix, they did that to us one day, and the next day we dropped our home-delivery prices on the street and just left them there, which forced them down on all home-delivery sales. That was a good way of getting our competitors' attention, letting them know they weren't going to outprice us.[14]

According to Norman, the feeling on the management team was that to continue leading the market in Tucson, Shamrock would have to grow substantially until it could compete with the large national companies whose local plants were in the Salt River Valley in Maricopa County. As time passed, it became even clearer to him that more than growth, survival was at stake. Reaching this conclusion followed a close look at Shamrock's market position vis-`a-vis its major competitors.

In the early 1950s when the company began expanding outside of Tucson and into other parts of southern Arizona, Shamrock's product line was still incomplete, compared to the competition. In particular, Carnation had a complete line of milk, cultured products, ice cream, and novelties; whereas Shamrock sold only fluid milk products and had begun making cottage cheese, buttermilk, and sour cream on only a limited basis. Overall, Shamrock was at a disadvantage in expanding into a fully competitive cultured product line from its Tucson base. The reason: as milk had to be hauled to Tucson at the producers' expense, Shamrock simply could not attract producer milk at a price competitive with that offered by plants in the Phoenix area. Conversely, Shamrock's Phoenix competitors had an important advantage in the retail pricing of product. They could serve a customer in southern Arizona at a very competitive price and at the same time sell customers in the Phoenix area at a less competitive price. This would not only take volume away from Shamrock but, long term, threatened to impair its ability to operate at a profit. Since Shamrock served only southern Arizona, it was not in a position—yet—to retaliate in other parts of the state.

For Norman it seemed obvious that Shamrock's dominance in southern Arizona would be eroded little by little as the market grew. In order to secure its future, Shamrock needed to broaden its product line, to make milk products more competitively, and to operate statewide. Said Norman, "The decision to build a processing plant in the Phoenix area became not only an obsession but a necessity."[15]

NORMAN McCLELLAND

During the time we were building the plant, we were bottling milk in Tucson and hauling it to Phoenix in trailers. That was in 1955 and early '56, and the amount of milk we were distributing in Phoenix was relatively small compared to our total volume. Underlying everything was our knowledge that Phoenix was where the business was in the state. Plus the fact that there wasn't enough volume in the Tucson market to warrant our marketing cottage cheese or ice cream very successfully. If we were ever going to amount to very much, we needed a plant in Phoenix....All of us in management had sleepless nights, but we knew we had to be there, even though getting there represented an irreversible commitment of a small company's total resources.

After we had purchased the land, drawn up plans for the new plant, and were about to sign the building contract, I made a point of asking Dad and Mother if they were still absolutely certain we should move ahead. Both of them indicated without equivocation that there would be no turning back. They knew everything was on the line, but felt they would rather lose it all than consider quitting in midstream. Their commitment and support reinforced my own determination, and that of others in management, to give it all we had and to succeed. Dad was always results-oriented, and in the final analysis the results were favorable: We made money. So from his point of view we did the right thing. It was his feeling that if your plans were right and if you executed them properly, you should meet your objective. And we did.

I was the one who found the land, but Dad was up here quite a bit, and he did put his stamp on the project. We spent $50,000 to buy ten acres of what was just sheep meadow then. But we knew a freeway was coming. That's why we chose this location—to be on the highway. We built the plant on the front end of the property and designed it so we could expand to the west and a little to the north, which over time we've done. But the basic building, outside of a little addition we made to the front, is virtually the same as what we built in the fifties.

Initially, we were a small organization. John Harty, our general manager, arrived in Phoenix first to launch our sales effort, while we continued hauling product up from Tucson. When we moved to Phoenix, I ran the plant operation, Dave Hall managed the office, and we all got out and made sales calls. We were wearing a lot of hats. You'd go out and make sales calls all day and come back in and keep on working at night. And if you had plant problems, you'd work on those and then do the accounting. Eventually you went home, got something to eat, and went to bed for a while, then got up the next morning and did the same thing again. With a small business, just getting started, you couldn't afford to hire anyone else.

Dave and his wife had an apartment in Phoenix, and often I'd use their spare room—we were very thrifty at that point. I'd be here three or four days a week. Then the company began maintaining its own apartment, which I shared with two other Shamrock people until '66 or '67, when I finally moved my family to Phoenix. Initially, it was just David and me, and maybe fifteen others in the plant operation. John Harty acted more like a sales manager than a general manager, first in running the retail aspect of sales and later the wholesale.[16]

Bill Boyce, Shamrock Dairy's reliable field man and a mentor not only to Dave Hall but also to Norman and, years later, his son, Kent, said he was convinced that Norman was a visionary. "He could see ahead—because when we came up here and broke into this market, I'd have sworn ninety-nine to one that we would fail. We were up against all those big dairies, and we were itty-bitty. What happened was that they made mistakes and we didn't."[17]

In late October 1956 the new milk-processing plant officially opened, and all of Phoenix was invited to tour the operation during four days of festivities. Two hundred thousand people responded to a $20,000 radio, TV, and newspaper advertising campaign that promised free entertainment, free dairy samples, door prizes, games of chance, carnival rides, and prizewinning Guernsey cattle on display in an improvised show ring. According to John Underwood, who

created the in-house *Shamrock News* and masterminded all of the company's promotional campaigns for twenty years, "The grand opening put us on the map in
Phoenix. It was a really big event for this community."[18]

DAVID BOYER HALL
Senior Vice President of Shamrock Foods Company

Norman and I often reminisce about how we came to Phoenix
and paid cash for the land, paid cash for the equipment in the plant,
went out and purchased a fleet of trucks—also with cash. Then we
went out and solicited customers. Of course, we were twenty-eight
years old at the time; certainly, if we were to do that today, we would
do it exactly in reverse—either acquire a company or leverage it by
financing. Instead, we paid cash outright for just about everything.
I've often thought how lucky we were, because none of the competition considered us a threat. Borden Company had a dilapidated
plant in Phoenix but was not motivated to upgrade it. I believe that
it was D. V. Welsh of Borden who made the remark, "Well, those
young guys out there, they built this new plant and in six months I'll
be able to buy it for a song because they won't be in business anymore." We were able to get a darn good toehold in Phoenix and a
darn good volume going through our plant before anybody said,
"Hey, those kids are going to be here in business." Had they gone
after us at the outset and prevented us from getting volume, we
might not have succeeded. On the other hand, if we had all looked
at things from a more mature business point of view, I'm sure we
would have done everything differently.

I think the real reason we succeeded was that everybody worked
very hard. I can remember the first seven years we were here. We
always worked on Saturdays, and I used to come out and cut the
lawn on Sundays. When we first opened the plant, we were the only

building out here surrounded by sheep. John Harty and I would have fits because no sooner would we leave work at 5 P.M. than there would be a thousand sheep eating that beautiful lawn of ours. Overall, the amount of work we each did was unreal. We always took work home at night—because we had to. None of us thought anything of it because, well, that was our job.

Coming up to Phoenix was Norman's idea. It was the kind of decision that would make or break the company. And he made it work. And by making it work, he gave us all a lot of confidence.[19]

Norman always insisted that the expansion to Phoenix was inevitable: "I think we knew all along that it was the right thing to do, but I also think we had a little question as to whether we could ever make a profit. What we had going for us was that we were a highly profitable organization in Tucson, and we continued to do well there, which helped us in starting Phoenix. We knew we could sustain some losses if we had to."[20] Yes, there were some losses, but, said Dave Hall, "I know for a fact that we started up in August 1956 and the month of November was profitable."[21]

Had Norman ever felt any pressure from his parents, particularly his father? "I guess I did, early on. Being part of the family, growing up on the property, then joining the company, assuming responsibility, and eventually taking charge of the whole operation, I did have a need to prove myself in those first years of expectation. What I particularly learned from my dad was the importance of being first."

"I remember an expression he had: *el fronte*. Each day he would ask the route salesmen who stopped by his office if they were on *el fronte*. The term had a powerful meaning for him, for it was said that when a cow has twins, the stronger calf is always on the cow's front udder. In asking the question, Dad wanted to know if his salesmen were outselling the competition that day. Ultimately, being number one, the strongest, became synonymous with the name Shamrock."[22]

Mr. Mac lived on for a dozen years following the opening of the Phoenix plant. He was seventy-six years old when he died—of heart failure, according to Frances.

FRANCES McCLELLAND

By the time Dad died, Mother, too, was pretty much out of the company's day-to-day operations. She first showed signs of having Parkinson's disease when Dad lost his leg. That was the first time I noticed anything, about 1960. She wasn't too bad for probably five years; then she started going downhill until she really couldn't take care of herself anymore and died in 1977. In her last few years she did not have great quality of life. She was well cared for, and she was a very easy patient, but she couldn't hold a lengthy conversation because she couldn't remember too well. She had always enjoyed working in the office, more than keeping house. She did whatever had to be done, at home and at the office, but she really liked office work better.

We had moved to downtown Tucson in 1942, and eventually I built a house for the three of us, about twenty blocks north of where we had been living. The design was unusual, in that they had their place and I had mine. My apartment joined on at the service porch so I had access to the dining room and kitchen, but I had my own living room. Both Dad and Mother lived there until they died. Eventually I built another house in Tucson—for me.[23]

The company mourned the passing of each of its cofounders, but its traditions continued and have remained unchanged. Foremost among its values, long established and strictly adhered to, are these:

•Every employee is part of one great team, not only working together but dependent on one another and sharing in the company's success.

•The first priority for each member of the team is to serve the customer with quality products and service at the lowest possible cost.

•To be competitive, the company must grow faster than the market, and such growth must bring commensurate earnings.

•A sense of integrity prevails in the company along with a spirit of loyalty— the loyalty of the company to the employee and the loyalty of the employee to the company.

These were the cornerstones of Shamrock's success as the country's ninth largest institutional food distributor, and also part of the company culture, from the very beginning.

Chapter Two

Mr. and Mrs. Mac

"There's a quiet sweetness in the Irish," Norman once said, "and it comes from the land itself, I believe, where the only sounds are the occasional cries of gulls and, less frequently, of a cow wanting to be milked."[1] In Northern Ireland the land within the glacier-made saucer surrounding Lake Neagh was a patchwork of farmlands and pasturelands in the decades leading up to the turn of the twentieth century. It was characteristic of British agriculture at the time for nearly 85 percent of the farmland to be landlord owned and rented out to farmers as tenants. Such a family were the McClellands of County Down. The farm they tenanted was at Cloughenramer, near Newry, a town that bordered the river Bann midway on its journey from Lake Neagh to the Atlantic Ocean.

Potatoes, barley, wheat, and oats grew in the loamy fields, set off from each other across the rolling landscape by hedgerows and stone ditches. It was on such a farm that William Thomas McClelland was born on October 22, 1891, the first of three children.

WILLIAM THOMAS "W. T." MCCLELLAND
Cofounder of Shamrock Dairy

My parents owned the sixty-acre farm. When I say "owned," I mean they owned what was known as the "tenant right" at that time. The landlord had to be paid rent yearly, but as long as the rent was paid within a reasonable time, you could not be evicted. There were sheep, pigs, turkeys and chickens on the farm, and we kept twenty cows, such as they were, mostly dual purpose. They would give quite a flow of milk for a short time. I would venture to to say that their yearly average production was 200 pounds of butterfat, or maybe even less.[2]

The McClelland family had a contract to supply milk to the Poor Farm, in nearby Newry, which W. T. said was commonly called a home for the aged. He remembered that the contract price for supplying milk was ten cents in the spring and twelve cents in the winter for an imperial gallon, which was approximately one and a quarter American gallons.

A sturdy young man of medium height with blue eyes and pale brown hair, W. T. managed to receive an elementary-school education but spent most of his time working the farm. And the work was constant. As the farm had but one team of horses, it was necessary to find additional means of delivering to the Poor House, about three miles distant, when the team was in use planting in the spring and harvesting in the fall. During those two very busy seasons, W. T. said that it became "one of my unpleasant duties to borrow the neighbor's donkey and deliver the milk, mornings and evenings after school."[3]

At age seventeen, by which time both of his parents had died, he inherited the family's tenant rights, according to Irish law, as he was the eldest son. With help from his sister, Margaret, and brother, David, he assumed management of the farm. To maintain their tenancy, all three worked very hard.

Seeking to expand his horizons and not content to remain in County Down, after four years of management W. T. decided to sublet the farm and immigrate to America. He bypassed the usual urban immigrant ghettos of New York and Boston and went straight to Arizona. He had an uncle, A. W. Smith, who lived in Tucson, where he hoped to find work, and when he arrived he got a job as a ranch hand at the Triple C Ranch in the nearby community of Oracle.

It was 1912, the year Arizona ceased being a territory and entered the Union as the forty-eighth state. Thus it was as much a turning point for the place in which he settled as it was for the young Irish immigrant himself. A year after his arrival he did move to Tucson, where he would spend most of his life, and took a job with Henry Peterson, who had acquired the Holstein Dairy. For three years he was a dairy hand and milk deliveryman. Then he took temporary leave of Tucson and returned to Ireland to dispose permanently of his interest in the family farm. He also made an appropriate settlement with his sister and brother.

As it turned out, concluding a business transaction was but one success of W. T.'s return trip to Northern Ireland. Revisiting his homeland gave him an opportunity to become acquainted with Sara Winifred Parker, who lived on a thirty-five-acre farm at Ballykeel, some distance from Cloughenramer but within reach of the town of Newry. W. T. and Winifred were related by marriage and, indeed, were introduced to one another by their respective families. Her uncle, Sam Wright, was married to W. T.'s half-sister, Minnie Wright, a child from his father's first marriage.

Born in 1894, Winifred was one of six children, all of whom were pressed toward higher education and high ambitions by their parents, James and Jane Parker. Winifred attended local schools with her sisters and brothers, then, at age eighteen, went off to Dublin to earn a teaching degree at the Marlborough Training College. Later, she taught school for five years, first in County Davan, then in more familiar territory, County Down.

In January 1917, W. T. returned to Arizona and the Holstein Dairy, remaining there until the United States entered World War I. He enlisted in the army that September, and after the prescribed military training was shipped to France as a member of the American Expeditionary Forces. He wore his uniform with the same pride with which he regarded his newly received citizenship, a benefit of his enlistment. After the armistice was signed in November 1918, W. T. stayed on in Europe, serving in the army of occupation in Germany until late 1919.

On postwar leave before returning to the United States, he made another visit to County Down and spent serious time with Winifred Parker. The two now agreed to correspond when, after being discharged from the army, W. T. settled once more in Tucson and returned to work at the Holstein Dairy. When the opportunity arose for him to purchase the small Modern Dairy from George C. Woods, in 1920, he went into business for himself.

Letters between him and Winifred crossed the ocean frequently. As everyone in the family must have known, a long-distance courtship was taking place. When she finally left Northern Ireland with her brother, Bill Parker, in December 1920, her plan was to immigrate to Arizona and marry W. T. McClelland. "We arrived the day after Christmas," Bill Parker remembered, "and Winnie was married the following day."[4] The ceremony over, Bill moved on, traveling west to California and a promised job with Joseph Wright, an uncle who owned a grocery store in Sausalito, just north of San Francisco. "It was part of the arrangement," said Parker. "He had paid half of my fare."[5]

Although W. T. McClelland had become a naturalized American and a patriot as well, his Irish sensibilities remained with him always, never dimming. Not surprising was his choice of a bride from the Emerald Isle he had left behind but never truly abandoned. For him she would be a lifelong reminder of County Down's quiet serenity. That serenity may have shaped Winifred's personality, but it would not long govern her life; for the land that greeted her when she settled in America bore no resemblance to the land she had always known.

County Down had been rainy and damp, with lush fields and distant green hills, and there was an all-pervading tranquillity that seemed untouched by time. Arizona, by contrast, was flat and arid, with occasional dry mountains, and the roads were lined with desert brush, mesquite, and prickly pear. But the once-dedicated schoolteacher now became a zealous pioneer; it seemed an effortless transition for someone with her easygoing nature.

Where she had formerly ridden a bicycle to make the trip from farm to town, she now learned to drive a car—on dusty, unpaved roads that turned to ribbons of bumpy corduroy on those rare occasions when it rained. Mostly, however, the weather was idyllic, almost ideal for cattle raising and the production of milk, according to Shamrock's longtime cattle-breeding consultant.

CLIFF KNIGHT

Arizona is one of the good states for production. It's certainly better than a midwestern or northeastern state with all their climate and water problems and moisture. The disadvantage Arizona has is our very hot summers—in July, August, and part of September particularly. The heat knocks production and cuts down on fertility in the animals. However, the other nine or nine and a half months are very good for production. We have high-quality feed available, and I'd certainly rather be in Arizona and deal with those problems than face the snow and wet weather in other parts of the United States.[6]

For Winifred, Arizona seemed a land of perennial summer, and she longed to wear her straw hat even in winter. But the dictates of fashion, and a word of advice from a friend, finally convinced her that straw hats were summer gear, even in the heated climate of Tucson.

In the early 1920s, Tucson was a town of little more than 20,000 residents, with a small but steady stream of new arrivals continually increasing that number. Many new arrivals were drawn by the clean, dry air and almost endless sunshine that were thought to cure a whole range of respiratory ills. Tent colonies for victims of tuberculosis dotted the region, and dude ranches proliferated to such a degree that Tucson came to be known as the dude-ranch capital of the United States. Automobile ownership in Tucson, and throughout the state, was high— Arizona was said to be ninth in the nation in per capita car ownership. But what proved the major impetus for business growth occurred when the Southern Pacific Railroad strung tracks down through the Santa Cruz Valley to meet the railhead for the Southern Pacific de Mexico at Nogales.

Despite the ongoing growth and continued promise offered by the region, this was not the best of times for Arizona's agrarian community. A relentless drought discouraged many farmers who were trying to keep undernourished cattle alive. It was not surprising, then, that after a year of dairy ownership the McClellands accepted an offer from M. S. Autrey, who had originally started the Holstein Dairy, to purchase their Modern Dairy holdings. Freed, for a time, from the burden of ownership, they decided to try their luck in California, moving to the Long Beach area just south of Los Angeles. They barely had time to unpack, however, for in the fall of 1922 they received word that Autrey was not maintaining his payment schedule and they would have to take back the business. The McClellands returned to Tucson, where they would remain for the rest of their lives.

Reacquiring Modern Dairy was a joint effort by the McClellands, who immediately relocated it to a parcel of land W. T. had purchased on his own in 1919, about seven miles northwest of downtown Tucson. The new operation, situated on the south bank of the Rillito River at what became the intersection of Ruthrauff and Romero roads, was a twenty-four-hour-a-day challenge. The McClellands started out with only twenty cows and one Model T Ford truck, and they did all the milking, bottling, and delivering themselves. At that time there were twenty dairies operating in Tucson and fifty-four in the Phoenix area, all competing for business.

"Mother and Dad built a small adobe house at the dairy," said Frances. "It had a living room, dining room, kitchen, one bedroom and bath plus a sleeping porch. Later they built two frame houses and an office nearby."[7] The McClellands started out with fewer than fifty customers, whom they served twice daily. Like most dairy farmers then, they worked long hours every day, seven days a week. There were no days off and no time for holidays. Every twelve hours they milked the cows, bottled the milk, and delivered it immediately. As Frances recalled, "Both my parents had a very strong work ethic."[8]

For W. T., life in rural Arizona was not unlike what he had experienced in County Down; the rigors of farming were altered very little by geography. He had dealt with farm animals since childhood and had learned dairy management from earlier jobs. For his bride, running a dairy farm was similarly reminiscent of her childhood; it was also a total departure from her education, training, and experience, but she quickly found it her métier. Frances recalled that her mother "had a very good mind and was a whiz at figures. She could add a column of numbers in the wink of an eye."[9]

Eager to help the business succeed, Winifred assumed the duties of book-keeper. She not only kept the accounts and managed the office but when an extra pair of hands was sometimes needed, she even helped with the bottling of milk and the endless washing routine. She contributed equally to establishing the new enterprise, but, according to Bill Parker, "it was our mother who came up with the name for the new dairy. Mother and Mac had been corresponding for some time. When he wrote that he and Winnie were starting a dairy and needed to name it, Mother didn't have to be asked twice."[10]

Her suggestion: Shamrock Dairy, taking its name from the Irish national emblem. It proved an apt appellation and its image a perfect symbol of the company's philosophy. As described later by a senior employee, "The three leaves of the Shamrock form a natural design. One leaf represents the officers and administration, one leaf represents the employees, and the third leaf represents the customers. Each leaf needs the others to complete the ideal of a rewarding enterprise. It is the complete harmony represented by all three leaves that forms the Shamrock image."[11]

The task of running a dairy operation proved so demanding that within a couple of years another pair of hands was sorely needed. Earl Bates came to work in the plant where milk was processed, then he became the first hired routeman. His wife recalled that Earl "used to go out at eleven o'clock in the morning and then delivered the evening milking at eleven at night—he would just leave it at each door."[12] The fresh raw milk was bottled in pints and quarts, and Earl would start his home delivery route right after the milkings. At that time the retail selling price was twelve cents a quart, delivered.

From the beginning, the business was committed to delivering quality products, providing good service, and operating with efficient management. Careful attention was paid to cleanliness. "The one word I think best characterized my father was 'integrity,'" Frances observed.[13]

The dairy's initial success could be attributed as much to the dynamics of the McClelland partnership as to the owners' penchant for toil. For Earl Bates and for the thousands of employees who followed him, the man he reported to was not W. T., William T. or Mr. McClelland, but simply Mr. Mac. And, logically, the other half of the management team—although called Winnie by her husband—was widely known as Mrs. Mac. That is how they were referred to, and that is how they continued to be recognized as their business and family dynasty began to grow.

Chapter Three

Flip of a Coin

66 *T*he dairy and I are almost the same age,"[1] Frances McClelland always said. "Then when I was about three years old, I put in a request to my parents that I wanted a little brother. And lo and behold, in due time I got a little baby brother. That was a happy event in my life, and I have to say that rarely, if ever, have I regretted it."[2]   Norman was born in 1927, when Frances was four. The two of them spent their childhood at the dairy, where they lived.

FRANCES McCLELLAND

It was pleasant around the dairy. We had green lawns and trees, and in the evenings we'd sit outside, particularly in the summertime, and our friends would come out and visit. We were probably about half an hour from town—it would be only fifteen minutes now— and the trip could be treacherous, particularly when it rained. Our life there was very simple. We used to play in the fields and ride the cows; we were always warned to stay away from the bulls. There was a silo that we would climb and dare each other to jump off into, and I remember Norman's having a treehouse at one time.

Between the first house we lived in at the dairy and the plant itself was an orchard where there were apricot and peach trees. Every summer Mother would preserve fruit and make jam. North of this orchard was the lane that ran to the plant. South of the house there were pepper trees. I also remember hollyhocks growing; Mother and Dad planted a lot of flowers.

My dad and I were quite close when I was a girl. Traditionally, the first child bonds with the father, so I was my Daddy's girl. He had a name for each of us. Mother was the Old Mick, Norman was the Young Mick, I was the Big Mick. Dad was not particularly affectionate, but neither was Mother. That was just not part of their nature. They never talked about feelings. They were not demonstrative, but you just knew that they loved you.

I would say that Norman and I had a fairly normal childhood out there in the country. We were raised according to a kind of Irish philosophy: "Children were to be seen but not heard." So we were not encouraged to participate in family discussions or anything like that, as children are now. People tend to think of the Irish as volatile, but the McClellands were more contained, and Mother was a very kind, gentle person; she was a Parker, after all, and they were very gentle people. Mother in particular lived by the rule: what would the neighbors think? It didn't matter that we didn't have any neighbors—what would *anybody* think? Very definitely, you had to put up a good front.

Day after day, Mother worked right along with Dad. Anything she considered right for Dad or the dairy was something she was interested in. He might have been off somewhere, tending to his cows, but she was always around. He was very fond of animals. He'd go out every morning and talk to his cows and pat them. If he were to meet somebody new who said her name was Anne, he would say, "Oh, I have a cow by the name of Anne." People weren't quite sure how to take that. He had a wry sense of humor but a quick temper. Because he was honest and fair, his employees always respected him.[3]

Dan Jones, who joined Shamrock in 1937 and worked in the milk plant for seven years before assuming his first delivery route, recalled Mr. Mac as being "very firm and very blunt"—fair with his employees but gentle and caring where his herd was concerned.[4]

DANIEL "DAN" JONES
Retired Tucson employee

Mr. Mac always loved working with the calves. He weaned them himself. He would come out in the afternoon or the morning and go down to the fields and call those cows. Pretty soon they would come up to the corrals. In 1937 or '38, when we had a big flood, water inundated the power supply and the electricity went off. We had to milk the cows by hand for several days. I remember Mr. Mac's coming out to help us. He didn't need to do that, but he did. It took a long time to milk fifty or sixty cows by hand.[5]

"When I first started working for the dairy, things were very primitive," recalled Lamar Sherman, who began his career at Shamrock in 1943. "Mr. Mac hired me as a milker, then after about a year I became a herdsman."[6] Milking, processing, storing, transporting—all of it was done by hand in the early decades of Shamrock history. Hours were long and the work was demanding, and though living at the dairy was far from plush, it was never unhappy.

NORMAN MCCLELLAND

It was the best life, growing up on the farm. It was our playground, and we spent a lot of time by ourselves growing up. We were given the run of the place pretty much and expected to show up at dinnertime, but in between there weren't too many questions asked, which was pretty nice. At various times Dad tried different crops in some of the fields to the north of our house. I remember his raising corn in one of them, and in another there was a black walnut tree. Dad was fond of animals, so we had chickens and ducks. At one time we even had pigs; they usually managed to get out at dinnertime.

I can remember, as a youngster, irrigated farmland, cattle on pasture, milking cattle, and all of the chores associated with life on the farm—from caring for the animals to helping in the milk-bottling operation. The milking barn was a very small facility. Raw milk was carried from it by hand in metal containers across a road into another building where it was poured and pumped up over an aerator, cooled, and put into a tank where it was pasteurized. Then it was bottled in glass. The cases were iced, and the product was delivered in open-sided delivery trucks.

My father kept wanting me to work on the farm, but Mother was always kind of protecting me, saying, "He'll have plenty of time to work all his life. Let him just grow up." I respected my father, but I felt a lot closer to Mother. Dad was fair but really tough-minded. It was either black or white with him. Mother was always sort of the mediator. Frances and Dad were true McClellands. They shared the same personality. They would blow up at each other, and Mother would have to intercede. I had something of the Parker personality, which was more like, "Let's calm down now and see what we can figure out here." That's the kind of family we were.[7]

"There was no discrimination in our house," Frances remembered. "Norman had to help with the dishes just as I did, and we would each take turns. It kind of evolved that Norman eventually did the washing and I did the drying, because when I washed, the dishes kept being rejected."[8]

Like other dairies in the area, Shamrock built its business on the bottling and delivery of raw milk, but with the outbreak of a typhoid epidemic in the early '20s, a major revision in the process was mandated. In October 1925, when the dairy was just three years old, Tucson's city council adopted what it called a complete milk-pasteurization ordinance. Years later, Robert Gromko, vice president of operations for the dairy division, described pasteurization as "the treatment that kills disease-producing bacteria. We heat the milk to 161 degrees and hold it for sixteen seconds at that temperature."[9] In the 1920s, of course, the process was much slower.

According to Milton Sivesind, capping a thirty-year career at Shamrock as a dairy and food plant engineer, "At Shamrock in the late twenties, milk was heated by steam pumped through the jacket of a 150-gallon stainless-steel vat, held at a temperature of 143 degrees Fahrenheit for a minimum of thirty minutes, then cooled over a surface cooler to under 50 degrees Fahrenheit and bottled immediately in sterile bottles. By 1940 a continuous system called high-temperature short-time pasteurization began to be popular. Two years later, Shamrock became the first dairy in Arizona to use the HTST system."[10]

That Shamrock had responded so quickly to the pasteurization mandate was commendable. However, they did so not because of the new ordinance but, as Jack Underwood remembered it, because of the loss of a wager.

JOHN C. "JACK" UNDERWOOD JR.
Former Vice President in charge of advertising and promotions

Mr. Mac flipped a coin with Henry Peterson, who owned the Holstein Dairy, where he had once worked. They were friends, but he lost the toss, so he had to put the pasteurizer in at Shamrock and also pasteurize the milk for Peterson. Well, then, Peterson just kept going downhill, and finally Mr. Mac took him out of business. Then he took the old Yale Dairy out of business. He was very tough.[11]

29

Buck Roberts was fresh out of the University of Arizona when he was hired by Shamrock as a milk tester. According to his wife, Mary Lorene "Cossie" Roberts, "He was one of the best judges to graduate from the university. Buck would sometimes go with Mr. Mac when he was buying cows and help him make the choices."[12]

LORENE "COSSIE" ROBERTS
Wife of a former dairy supplier and longtime McClelland family friend

Peterson's dairy was in financial trouble in 1934 and had gone into foreclosure. Buck didn't come home one night, and I was very worried about him. When he finally did get home, the next morning, he said that he and Mr. Mac had been milking Peterson's cows. It seems that the cows had been sold but were not going to be picked up until the following day. Buck and Mr. Mac hated to see the cows suffer, so they went over and milked them. I don't know about Mr. Mac's hands, but Buck's were all swollen.[13]

The Holstein Dairy acquisition took place in 1934 when Henry Peterson died. Yale Dairy was purchased three years later. Each acquisition exemplifed a Shamrock tradition, begun in the company's infancy, of planned expansion through acquisition. "We usually acquired the customer routes, maybe some trucks and some plant equipment, if there was any of it we could use," Frances noted. "Normally we didn't buy the building or the land. And we've never bought many cows."[14] "Mainly we bought the distribution," Dave Hall explained. "We would buy a company's assets, and pay a good price for them, but we didn't buy its indebtedness. That would have to take care of itself."[15]

Some acquisitions yielded important personnel additions, however. For example, W. W. Dearing came aboard from Holstein Dairy when it was purchased by Shamrock and distinguished himself by focusing on developing cultured products. When Shamrock eventually shifted operations to Phoenix, he spent time there training plant people in the production of buttermilk, sour cream, and cottage cheese.

Treatment of milk by pasteurization was a major step for dairies in the mid-'20s, for it gave them a scientific basis for advertising safe milk. What followed was even more significant: the Standard Milk Ordinance, which was worked out on a national scale by members of the U.S. Public Health Service, dairy experts from several universities and from the industry itself, plus public health physicians and representatives from municipal health offices countrywide. The city of Tucson adopted the Standard Milk Ordinance in April 1927 and began putting its provisions into effect immediately. Shamrock Dairy was one of the first to meet the requirements, thereby enhancing its reputation for quality product and commendable service.

As a result of business and work-load increases, Shamrock had been forced to add a second retail delivery route in 1925, hiring additional employees to handle the volume. A third route was added in 1928. That was the year Mr. Mac first expressed an interest in owning Guernsey cattle. Milt Sivesind recalled that "Mr. Mac told me he went to Wisconsin and bought some Guernseys around West Salem and Westby along about that time."[16] Those purchases marked the beginning of his lifelong attachment to that beautiful breed of cattle and respect for the quality of milk they produced.

A minor milestone was reached in 1930 when Shamrock Dairy installed its first automatic bottle filler and the first bottle washer, devices that relieved milk handling of much of its drudgery. More important, the mechanical means of performing the routine work further ensured sanitary conditions within the milk-processing areas. "I remember the day the first bottle washer was installed," said Lavona Hawkins, who had regularly helped Mrs. Mac with housework and, occasionally, with office chores until she married John Hawkins, a milk tester in the plant. "Mr. Mac wanted to try out the bottle washer first, and when he did, he got his nose cut. He made light of it, though; he said if we thought his nose looked bad before, that cut wasn't going to help the looks of it at all."[17]

A major change in the management of Shamrock Dairy came in 1933 when Bill Parker, Mrs. Mac's younger brother, arrived from California to become a part owner and key player in the growing enterprise. He was the brother who, at age twenty-one, had accompanied his sister to Tucson from their family home in Northern Ireland. After more than twelve years in America, he had been invited to join the McClellands in running their dairy.

William Joseph Parker was far from the stereotypical Irishman. Rather than being boisterous and quick tempered, he was quiet and easygoing. Like his sister, he had a temperate demeanor and seldom became ruffled. His was the typical Parker coloring—dark brown wavy hair and dark brown eyes. He had grown up on the family farm, the fifth of six children. There had always been plenty of work and rarely much time for play. When he was a boy, most of the farm work was done by hand—cutting and gathering hay, tying sheaves of grain and forking the potatoes from the loam. "When I was ten, we got together with three families and bought a potato digger that was horse drawn," he remembered. "A little bit later we bought a two-horse mowing machine, which replaced the scythes we'd been using."[18]

WILLIAM JOSEPH PARKER
Former Chairman of the Board and brother of Mrs. Mac

Until I was twelve years old, I attended a local grammar school. It was a one-teacher school. Then I went to school in town, which was three miles away. Sometimes I would bicycle and other times I would walk. That was for three years until I was sixteen. I don't think it was the equivalent of a high school education; it would have been more like junior high. Then I trained to be a law clerk, though that wasn't what I wanted to do. I wanted to fly and get into the British Flying Corps. I applied twice, but was turned down.

It was my mother who decided I should move to the United States with Winnie; I went on to my uncle's house right after she and Mac were married. My uncle had hopes that someday I might follow him in the grocery store. At that time the big chains were coming in, so it didn't look very promising. Winnie and Mac were expanding and asked if I would like to come and work with them. It was just what I wanted to do.

I arrived in August of 1933 and started working in September. I went out on the routes to learn each one of them. Then I started selling. I went around knocking on doors. I got the gas lists from the Tucson Sunshine Club and I would go out and call on all the new people. I also called on restaurants and stores. I never learned the plant or milk production because I never spent much time there. I helped by drawing plans and doing some designing for the plant and other building projects. Then Winnie and I went down to Cox School and took some bookkeeping. It wasn't long before I took over from Winnie, keeping all the books for the dairy.

When I came in 1933, the business was set up and incorporated at a value of $20,000. The dairy plant was an old adobe house made over. A little bit was added to make a cold room on the south end. Everything was wheeled out of the east end on a cart. The milk barn was directly north of the plant. It was set up to milk fifteen cows on each side. There was a silo north of the milk barn. The corrals were around the silo, and there was a lane leading down through the middle of the corrals. Actually, that land was a continuation of Romero Road.[19]

FRANCES McCLELLAND

Uncle was a thwarted architect. I think he really would have loved to have been one. He did all the planning for the buildings, the sketches and that sort of thing. That was his area, his love. He really enjoyed it.

Other than Mother and Dad, the only family I had in Arizona was Uncle. His first name was William and the Irish nickname was Willie, but I never liked the name Willie, so I just called him "Uncle." I didn't have many uncles—in Arizona, he was the only one—so that wasn't a problem. At work, of course, I used to call him Mr. Parker. It didn't sound right to say "Uncle" in an office. Like all of the Parkers, he was friendly and easy to get along with. He could meet people well. He was probably a little more outgoing than Mother.[20]

Norman always insisted that the opportunity to work with Bill Parker had been one of his incentives for joining the family business. As a young adult, after two years of military service and a chance to see some of the world, Norman had begun to appreciate some of the opportunities that Shamrock offered. "Also," he added, "I liked my uncle a lot."[21]

NORMAN MCCLELLAND

Bill Parker was a very good person to be around. He was sort of an idea guy. He wasn't out there milking cows all day and irrigating the pasture at night like Dad. My dad just worked like a horse. He was the tough guy in the business, the one who ran the credit operation. Uncle Bill ran the sales part of the business, and that's where we were when I got out of school.[22]

"My uncle was the right kind of person to be a partner to my father," said Frances. "They made a good team. Dad was more aggressive and the leader. Uncle had a very nice manner. He did the advertising, sales, and public relations, and Dad did the plant and the cows and the receivables. They must have sorted out where their skills were."[23] Mr. Mac, his wife, and her brother became the triumvirate that led Shamrock for the next thirty years. In recognition of their separate roles, Mr. Mac became known as "Mr. Inside" and Bill Parker as "Mr. Outside."

"I felt certain before I came aboard that Shamrock was going to grow," Jack Underwood recalled, "knowing the way Mr. and Mrs. Mac, and Bill Parker operated—plus the knowledge I had of the company itself. I just felt that it was going to keep progressing and couldn't do anything but go forward."[24]

Chapter Four

The Second Decade and Beyond

W hen she was eight years old, Frances McClelland contracted polio, or infan-
tile paralysis as it was called then, when the idea of a vaccine or an actual cure
was still only a distant hope. Although she was just a child, she was expected to
accept her illness with grace: "I was told by my mother that though I might not
like having polio, I shouldn't tell anybody that." [1]

Frances was given exercises at first and as much help as possible, but it was
decided ultimately that she should enter the care of a California orthopedist, Dr.
Leroy Lowman. She was transported to Los Angeles for treatment at Children's
Hospital. She actually lived there awhile, then boarded with the Fletchers, a
family whose home was near the hospital. While living in Los Angeles, Frances
attended several different schools, one of them—the Cambria School—for
handicapped children.

FRANCES MCCLELLAND

During the next five years I had several operations, among them
a spinal fusion and a muscle transplant, in an effort to help keep me
straight. And then I had several operations on one leg, which meant

another hospital stay each time. I also had repeated physio-therapy—heat massage and exercises—and pool therapy .

The treatment was fairly routine: Each Monday they would put the heat over my legs and massage and exercise them. On Tuesdays I would go to the pool, be placed on a platform and lowered into the water. What wasn't routine or very much fun was the surgery. Ether was the anesthetic of choice in those days; it was nasty stuff that always made me sick.

The effect of the illness was that I was paralyzed mostly on the right side—severely paralyzed in my right leg, pretty badly in my back and stomach, also to a degree in my right arm and left leg. I could walk short distances unaided at first, but eventually a brace was put on my back and right leg. I used crutches when I was young, then got rid of them for a few years. I went back on them not long ago because my balance wasn't very good.[2]

Frances remembered coming home to Tucson for a long visit with the family one summer, and once or twice a year they would travel to California to see her.

In those years I felt as though I had two lives. I had one with my family, when I was at home, and a different life when I was in California. It just seemed like I would close the door on one life and open the door on the other one. I guess I didn't have the kind of nurturing that I needed then, especially after having surgery. Nan Fletcher, the woman who took care of me, was not a particularly nur-turing woman. She was divorced, with two daughters quite a bit older than I was. She had a job in a photo studio but barely eked out a living. I don't think she had any extra energy, other than to cope with her life, yet she did do special things for me. I can remember her taking me, in a wheelchair, to the movies on a Saturday or

Sunday afternoon. The theater was fifteen or twenty blocks away, and she didn't own a car. Now that was above and beyond the call of duty, but she knew I loved movies. She really did try.

At the end of five years, having done everything they could for me, my doctors finally sent me home. I was fourteen years old when I came back to Tucson, and Norman was ten. I had to fit into the family again after being away such a long time. I remember being extremely bashful then, the kind of child who, if you even looked at me, I would duck my head.[3]

By the time Frances returned from California, Bill Parker had become an established part of the family and the family business. "Uncle and I were buddies when I was growing up," she said, "and even in later years we were really good friends."[4]

When Bill Parker arrived in Tucson, Shamrock was operating three retail routes and one wholesale route, and there were ten full-time employees. "We were not serving out of town when I first came here," he recalled. "At one time Tucson had an ordinance that all milk sold there must be processed within a fifty-mile radius of the city, so that eliminated the Phoenix dairies. They could come to the city limits but no farther. The law was ultimately disregarded—it wasn't a practical law at all—but we didn't serve anyone out of town until probably the 1940s."[5]

Shamrock Dairy was well positioned for growth in 1934, when James W. Ewing joined Bill Parker in the sales department. Like Bill, according to Milton Sivesind, "Jim obtained customers by running the gas list. Since everyone who moved to Tucson had to have the gas and lights turned on, Jim got their names each morning from Tucson Gas and Light, made a point of visiting them, and became their friend. It was not long before Shamrock began delivering milk to them."[6]

NORMAN McCLELLAND

Jim Ewing, Sr., was one of the catalysts that moved Shamrock into southern Arizona communities. Shamrock had developed good rapport with milk producers, had been paying premium prices for milk and attracting the Salt River Valley's top shippers. Jim made many friends among farmers and businessmen throughout Arizona. These producers had more milk than could be sold in their existing markets—Safford, Duncan, Clifton, and Morenci. Shamrock agreed to take all their milk and in exchange received help and backing from others in the Safford–Morenci farming and business community to expand dairy-product sales.

This arrangement not only proved an excellent opportunity for Shamrock but also assisted milk producers who needed an expanding market for their products. Eventually, because of Jim Ewing's leadership, Shamrock had the opportunity to expand into Ajo in Pima County, and Bisbee and Douglas in Cochise County. Shamrock's continued growth rested on additional foundations as solid as these.[7]

That same year, Willie Wilson came to work in the office. Her husband, Jim, was a deliveryman, and the Wilson family lived in Bill Parker's house at the dairy. When the work load became too heavy for Mrs. Mac to handle alone, Willie was asked if she would lend a hand. She had three young children, but because the office was so close to home, she felt she could work and still be nearby if problems arose. She agreed to help out for a few days, but those few days stretched to weeks and months. Eventually she became the office manager and remained with Shamrock for more than twenty-five years. She was the first secretary of the company's credit union.

In 1933, milking machines began to appear in Arizona dairies, Shamrock included, according to Ralph Van Sant, who did commercial milk testing for Dairy Herd Improvement, a state agency. At the time he first became acquainted with Mr. Mac, Shamrock Dairy had fewer than two dozen cows and was buying milk from a half-dozen producers. Although hand milking was perennially done in stalls, with cows confined in stanchions, Ralph recalled seeing milking parlors where up to five stalls were merged together. And, he said, "I can remember once in Maricopa County, where I was testing at a particular dairy, they fenced off a section of the field to milk the cows by hand. The milk was poured into a can through a screen."[8]

The cone cooler was a rather primitive device still in use in the early thirties. Ralph said that milk put in the top was cooled by ice water circulating under it "and then, at the bottom, would be the brine."[9] Routeman Daniel Jones explained that, at the time, Shamrock had "a big ice-making machine, which made hundred-pound ice blocks in trays set in a twenty-by-twenty-foot brine tank. You needed a pully to work the trays out of the brine. It was the night man's job to get the blocks ready. When he poured hot water on them and turned the trays upside down—which was like turning refrigerator ice trays over—the blocks would slide right out. The drivers could break up the ice as they wished. The brine tank came after 1937; before that we bought ice from the iceman."[10]

Frances said, "When I used to go to the plant as a child, one of the things I remember was the milk coming down over the cooling tower inside. As it ran down, it cooled, and as it got down to the bottom, some of the milk would freeze and there would be little icicles of frozen milk. It was fun to break off the icicles and eat them."[11]

At the time Ralph first began testing, production in Arizona averaged about 8,000 pounds of milk per cow for each test period, a number that would more than double during the next fifty years. "Once a month we sampled milk," he noted. "In the early days there were hand-calculated records for each cow. Then, for herd development, we would send a monthly report to the dairy owners. Now, everything is processed through a computer. We began using an electronic method of testing butterfat in 1973." [12]

In 1934, the first cream-top glass bottle was introduced. Its wide, bulb-like neck was just about right to contain the cream that rose to the top of each quart of pasteurized milk. The cream-top bottle became a Shamrock specialty because the rich Guernsey cream was so popular with customers who appreciated being able to see it. According to Ken Orchekowsky, who had a long career at Shamrock, mostly in retail sales, "There was constant competition with other companies to see which one's bottle had the deeper cream line, from the top of the bottle down." [13]

With a special spoon, provided by the dairy, the neck of the bottle could be closed so the cream could be poured off as needed, still leaving a substantial volume of milk and cream intact. Much of Shamrock's advertising and marketing centered around the cream-top bottle, with the dairy investing heavily to educate the public in recognizing and requesting this special container.

By 1937, with the acquisition of Yale Dairy, Shamrock's delivery system included nine routes, and 700 to 800 gallons of milk were being processed daily. In addition, table cream, whipping cream and small quantities of skim milk were sold. Cottage cheese and buttermilk were purchased from Webster Dairy in ten-gallon cans and repackaged for delivery by Shamrock.

Dan Jones, who joined the company that year, starting out in the dairy, was among the employees who would have long careers with Shamrock. Dan, who became the first president of the Shamrock Dairy Federal Credit Union, remembered that he earned ninety-nine dollars a month at first and worked seven days a week. Later, he took over a route and after more than thirty years retired from Shamrock. He said that he and the other employees helped campaign for Jim Ewing, Sr., who was first elected to the Arizona State Legislature in 1945.

Dan Jones

I worked near the cows first. That was when the old barn was still there, north of the plant, and we would take the milk over to the plant and pour it over the aerator. That is where the milk came trickling down.

Most of the time we worked twelve hours a day. When we started in the plant in the morning, we went through and got every-thing bottled in the cold room. Sometimes that would take up to twelve hours, sometimes sixteen hours if the plant broke down, and it broke down often, then. I remember the ceiling in the old plant being very low—I could reach up and touch it. In the summertime it was awful working in front of the bottle washer because of the steam. Most of the men took off their shirts and worked without them because it was so hot. [14]

Also in 1937, Shamrock acquired a major interest in the Frozenpure Ice Cream Company on North Fourth Avenue in Tucson, adding ice cream to the product line for the first time. It did not catch on, then, as a major part of Shamrock's business, so in 1942 Shamrock's interest in Frozenpure was sold, and ice cream products were not carried again until 1959.

Tokens used for the retail purchase of dairy products appeared on the scene in 1937 and remained in use for the next eighteen years.

Kenneth "Ken" Orchekowsky
Former Tucson dairy route delivery employee

Tokens were small metal disks of variously sized circular or square shapes. Each was a little different because each represented payment for a different product. A description of the product was imprinted on each token, which was sold to a customer in advance of delivery. The customer would leave whatever tokens were needed for the products requested. This practice helped keep the delivery people from losing money because of extended credit.[15]

The tokens were stacked in bundles of thirty, one for each day of the month (for product that was delivered daily), and secured with a piece of wire pulled through a hole in the center. Tokens were treated as money; they told the milkman exactly what the customer wanted and that it was all paid for.

In 1938 Shamrock began homogenizing milk, a process that had to be sold to a public grown accustomed to the cream-top bottle and its highly noticeable cream line. "It had been a big selling point to have a cream-line bottle," Dan Jones observed.[16] Homogenization assured a thorough and consistent blend of milk and cream, eliminating the necessity of shaking a bottle to create the desired mix. Though an attractive new square bottle was used to denote homogenized milk, it took some time for the product to win public acceptance.

Responding to the pressures of a rapidly expanding business, Shamrock Dairy began to consider building an addition to the Tucson plant. Business had increased steadily since the mid-1930s; there were now eight retail routes and four wholesale routes, and milk sold for fourteen cents a quart.

Active planning for the plant addition began in late summer of 1940, with the Pima County Health Department serving in an informal advisory capacity. A number of prominent dairymen as well as local and state health authorities also contributed their ideas and advice, but years of planning by Shamrock's management preceded the ground breaking. Throughout that planning period, Mr. Mac, Bill Parker, Jim Ewing, and John Hawkins worked with the Cherry Burrell Corporation, an Iowa-based seller of plant equipment that had just opened a branch in Los Angeles. Together they laid out the new addition and equipped it to include a milk receiving tank, a 2,000-gallon-capacity milk holding tank, milk scales, preheater, cream pasteurizer, milk cooler, bottle washer, can washer and bottle conveyer. When the addition was completed, in May 1941, it had the most up-to-date equipment obtainable before World War II.

By then the Shamrock family had grown to thirty-five employees and utilized fifteen trucks and cars. The dairy was milking eighty-five cows of its own, from which came about forty-five female calves each year, and the milk supply was augmented by output from several herds owned by other dairymen. Each day, some 1,800 gallons of milk were delivered to local residents, along with hundreds of pounds of cottage cheese, butter, ice cream and cases of eggs.

The new plant's grand opening was a two-day celebration, beginning on Saturday, May 17, 1941, and the public was invited to participate. The event included several radio quiz programs offering cash prizes, a written quiz contest with fifty-dollar prizes for the winners, and free refreshments—not surprisingly, ice cream bars and chocolate milk. Interested visitors were given tours of dairy buildings and the new processing plant. On Sunday, the largest model-airplane meet ever held in Tucson took place across from the Shamrock Dairy on a new flying field dedicated by the mayor, Henry C. Jaasted.

The public at large was invited to the grand opening, and special invitations were issued to local Boy Scout and Girl Scout troops and to schoolchildren throughout Tucson and Pima County. Young people were routinely part of Shamrock's public relations strategy; they were accorded special attention not only as future customers but also as future working citizens of the city and state.

With its new addition, Shamrock became the first dairy in the Tucson area to be considered a model design for the U.S. Department of Health. Not only was it to provide milk products for Tucson consumers but for the next several years Shamrock Dairy supplied approved products to the military. With Davis–Monthan Airfield nearby and other military installations not far away, including Marana Air Base to the west, the area's population base increased enormously. There was some concern, of course, that when the hostilities were over and the military was deactivated or dispersed the sudden decrease in population would depress business and turn Tucson into a ghost town. This never happened. The war years spurred the business expansion that followed, and the postwar population growth became almost explosive.

Modernizing the Tucson plant continued in 1942 with the installation of the new high-temperature short-time (HTST) pasteurizing system A Cherry Burrell Model J, it was Arizona's first positive pasteurizing system, capable of pasteurizing milk and other products at a rate of 800 gallons an hour. Milk flavor and keeping quality were enhanced, and heating and cooling costs were cut 80 percent by use of a regeneration system that brought about the universal pasteurization of all product that passed through the milk plant.

Another improvement, made about the same time, was the addition of two York flake ice makers to keep milk, cream, and other products cool and fresh on trucks during delivery to homes and stores. The new machines, in use for the next ten years, eliminated the need to chip ice by hand from those big blocks every day.

In October 1943 Mr. Mac entered into a partnership with Clyde F. Rowe, a friend and colleague who had been a dairy specialist for the University of Arizona. Clyde purchased 40 acres to add to the 160 that Mr. Mac had owned for six years near Chandler, about twenty miles southeast of Phoenix. They organized and ultimately operated Emerald Farms, with ninety-five dairy cows and two bulls comprising a major addition to Shamrock's production capabilities.

CATHERINE ROWE LINDBLOOM
Widow of Clyde Rowe

My husband and Mr. Mac got to know one another because they both liked to play poker. Clyde got into Mr. Mac's poker group, and they became personal friends as well as professional friends. Clyde was close to turning forty at the time and thought that if he wanted to move into private business, he'd better do it then. Mr. Mac made sure that we put enough money in so we wouldn't just pull out if the going got rough. We raised $7,500 in cash, which was quite a large sum for us. Mr. Mac obtained the rest of what was needed, but he also kept the business on a partnership basis. We bought the herd from Marion Chandler—the daughter of A. J. Chandler, who founded the Chandler community—but she kept out the calves so she could begin another herd. A year or two later she was back in business, marching those cows about eight miles down Arizona Avenue, right through Chandler.[17]

Emerald Farms was finally incorporated in 1961, and in 1967 the Rowes sold back their interest in the company, by which time, said Catherine, "we were milking 650 cows a day."[18]

With American involvement in World War II came gasoline and tire rationing. Shamrock cut back its deliveries to alternate days and only daytimes instead of delivering milk at night or in the wee hours of the morning. There were fifteen routes by the end of the war, with ten added in 1946 and ten more in 1947, in just two years doubling the number the company operated.

New to Shamrock Dairy in 1943—a Tucson newcomer attracted to the dairy industry—was Thomas A. Stafford, who operated two different routes during his first year with the dairy. In 1944 he was asked to assume the job of relief man. According to the *Shamrock News*, "Relief at the time meant plant, sales, janitor, gardener or whatever. This experience, at times not very enjoyable, was very valuable. Hours were no consideration. At one time all products were stacked case by case and all products were unstacked and loaded out case by case on conveyors without power except muscles.

"For a period of over six months [Tom Stafford] stacked and loaded out all Shamrock products. This meant reporting for work at 2 A.M. and possibly finishing up at 6 or 7 P.M. He was so tired that sleep was many times more necessary than food and dinner, so food was eliminated in favor of sleep."[19]

Tom was promoted to route foreman by the time Shamrock had twenty

Tucson routes, and in 1954 began working with John Harty to build new retail routes in Phoenix. In 1956 when Shamrock opened its new plant there, Tom was placed in charge of personnel statewide. He developed a number of training programs, particularly in management, advancing his conviction that if a person had the necessary qualities, they could be developed, but such qualities could not be transferred to every individual. He believed that having the right caliber people on board would assure Shamrock's continued growth and productivity, and he was exceptionally gifted in being able to recruit the right people. He had an instinct about people, and most of the time was proved right.

According to Henry Reading, who started at Shamrock working under him as a sales trainee, "Tom lived Shamrock every hour he was awake. A deep thinker with a remarkable vision of the future, he was extremely dedicated to his work and would take almost any steps that would help achieve success for Shamrock."[20] Tom Stafford was convinced that a company was only as good as its people, and as he rose through the management ranks in the postwar era, he put his own particular stamp on the company in the talented people he hired and trained.

W. T. McClelland

The McClellands' first home.

William Thomas and Sara "Winifred" Parker McClelland.

Sara "Winifred" Parker McClelland.

William Thomas "W. T."

Mrs. McClelland in front of Shamrock Dairy's first dairy plant.

William Joseph Parker, Mrs. Mac's brother and the McClellands'
partner in Shamrock Dairy, 1934.

Mr. McClelland in Shamrock's first panel delivery truck.

Shamrock employers, Tucson plant.

Norman Parker McClelland and calf.

Frances Helen McClelland astride cow.

Shamrock Dairy's prize-winning Guernsey herd.

Shamrock deliverymen in front of Tucson plant.

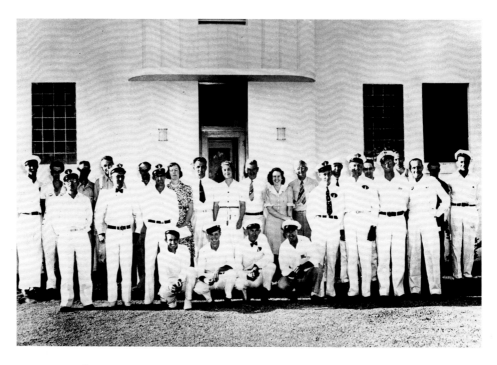

Shamrock's management and employees in front of the Tucson plant, 1941.

Exterior view of Tucson plant and offices.

Chapter Five

New Leadership, New Directions

*T*he year 1947 dawned with an array of plans to commemorate Shamrock's upcoming twenty-fifth anniversary. It would be a smoothly executed celebration designed to involve whole families, children as well as adults. "Jack Underwood was the man who became instrumental in getting crowds of people to the open house out at the dairy," Norman recalled.[1] Jack would not become a full-time Shamrock employee until the mid-'50s, but the company had become Jack's valued client in 1946, retaining him to collaborate with Bill Parker on much of its marketing and advertising plans.

Major events like the Christmas party were handily masterminded by Jack, as was the annual grocers' breakfast, for which, he noted, "we used to invite all the grocers and their employees to come to the dairy for a big Sunday breakfast. Sometimes we'd have up to three thousand people there and a crew outside cooking ham. The company, always quite community oriented, was willing to fund various promotions to strengthen public awareness of Shamrock."[2]

The 1947 event got under way with a barrage of newspaper ads and press releases announcing that for a quarter of a century Shamrock Dairy had supplied Tucson with rich, pure milk products—"healthful and wholesome food," the company proclaimed—whose uniformly high quality was affirmed by the fact that Shamrock dairy products had won top awards at the 1947 Arizona State Fair.

The state fair kudos were for grade-A pasteurized milk, grade-A table cream, grade-A buttermilk, and homogenized milk—blue ribbons won in competition with similar products from all other Arizona dairies. The twenty-fifth anniversary, recognized officially in late autumn, gave Shamrock the opportunity to draw attention to its prizewinning livestock, both male and female, which had been developed in the dairy's Guernsey breeding program. At the 1947 state fair, Bloom, Berry, Ellen and Luella made up Shamrock's First Prize Dairy Herd Group of show cattle, and first-place honors were also won by Bluebell, the senior calf and junior champion of 1947.

To underscore the cleanliness and efficiency of the dairy, Shamrock's advertising now regularly presented images of its cheerful routemen in uniforms—white shirt, white trousers, white cap with a black bill, dark belt, and dark shoes—that made them look every bit as wholesome as the product they delivered. Ads were created to remind customers that "Shamrock milk safeguards your health with its purity." This purity was protected by the green cellophane wrapping on the patented cream-top bottle.

The wrapper was designed to serve more than one purpose. First, it drew customer attention because of its emerald-green coloration. Second, it sealed out any possible contaminants that might have accumulated on a regular bottle cap. Just under the green wrapper on the cream-top bulb were the words "It Whips," and the cream could be seen easily right through the glass. Further, the Shamrock name, the shamrock motifs, and the image of a Guernsey cow that appeared on each bottle clearly identified the product, establishing a high degree of recognition all through southern Arizona that would persist despite the changes ahead.

The year 1947 not only occasioned Shamrock's twenty-fifth anniversary but also heralded the coming of waxed-paper containers. Shamrock adopted this carton for packaging its milk and cream, which almost immediately contributed to an increased volume of business. The carton had several advantages over glass bottles, among them the fact that they were lightweight, disposable, and not easily damaged. For a while, Shamrock products were sold in both paper

and glass containers, but eventually nonreturnable paper cartons won total acceptance. Customers were already pleased not to have to wash and return glass
bottles, especially in those outlying communities that were beginning to be
serviced in ever greater numbers by Shamrock Dairy.

With the coming of waxed-paper cartons, Shamrock installed a Pure-Pak
filling machine in its processing plant, and milk packaged by this machine began
being distributed to the Tucson market in 1947, the year Milt Sivesind joined
Shamrock as a plant worker.

MILTON "MILT" SIVESIND
Former Chief Engineer, Phoenix Dairy

The machine bottled quarts, pints, and half-pints in paper. Its
speed was thirty-five cartons per minute. It was the best paper
machine available, yet it was a crude contraption—we had lots of
cartons that leaked at the stapled top or the glued bottom. But it
produced a nonreturnable container that had beautiful advertising on
four sides, and storekeepers loved it. No empty glass bottle returns.[3]

The advent of the waxed-paper carton not only shifted the emphasis away
from glass containers but from the cream-top bottle as well. By then homogenized milk had become a fully accepted commodity. The war years had seen an
enormous increase in demand for dairy products in southern Arizona. Now Mr.
Mac and his growing work force saw an opportunity for even greater expansion.
"We'd had big growth during the war," Frances McClelland recalled. "A lot of
people had come to Tucson, and after the war a lot of them came back because
they liked the climate."[4]

The McClelland tradition, begun with Mr. Mac, had always been not to take
capital out of the company but to pour it back in—investing in cattle, new equipment, and new acquisitions. Still, the McClellands' personal income had grown
dramatically since the earliest days of Shamrock Dairy.

"COSSIE" ROBERTS

Mr. Mac was at our house one time—it was probably in the late forties. We were talking about the new income-tax laws, and suddenly he was telling us how much he had to pay. We were all astonished at the amount he mentioned. He came right back and said, "If you don't make it, you don't have to pay it, and they didn't take all I make. Look what I get with the money I give them, compared to what I get from other money I spend." Then he began to sing the praises of our country and all the rewards of living here. He was very patriotic.[5]

In the company's silver anniversary year, new milking facilities were built at what was then called Hill Farm, home to Shamrock's herd of Holstein cattle, located on a low rise near the Tucson plant. Later known as Shamrock Hill Farm, it increased not only the milking capacity but also the efficiency and economical mode of operation of the entire dairy.

In 1948 Frances McClelland joined Shamrock full time. She had graduated from the University of Arizona with a major in accounting, then worked two years as financial secretary for Tucson's Trinity Presbyterian Church. Actually, she said, she had "started working at the dairy in my teens. I would work during my time off during summer vacations, in the afternoons or anytime they needed me when I was not in school."[6] She attended St. Joseph's Academy (behind St. Joseph's Hospital), a girls' school in Tucson because, unlike Tucson High School, it didn't have stairs. When she came home from school, she was likely to find her mother not in the kitchen but in the office. She would call to find out what Mrs. Mac planned for dinner that evening, then get it started before her mother came home. Later, when she herself went to work in the dairy, she assumed responsibilities that were as varied as her mother's had always been.

FRANCES MCCLELLAND

I worked in the office doing deposits and figuring producers,
checked drivers in, worked on accounts receivable, occasionally
answered the phone, worked on recaps and eventually learned how
to post the various books of the company. Later on, I kept the transport books and the corporate books. Over the years I worked at
most of the office jobs in the company.[7]

I guess I was brainwashed. My mother could add a column of
figures in nothing flat. Both Norman and I inherited some of that, I
probably more than Norman. So it was a given fact at quite an early
age that I was going to the university to major in accounting; there
was never any question about it. And then I was going to go out and
earn thirty dollars a day, which was what accounting firms charged
per day. Back then, that was probably a lot of money.

There was a brief period when I was supposed to be studying to
become a CPA, but I am not one of those self-motivated people. I
need to be in some kind of discipline, so I never did that, and I don't
know that it was terribly essential for going on into the business. I
was always nudged along by my parents. They wouldn't let me sit in
the office and do an ordinary job. They knew I could do more, so
they pushed me, both Dad and Mother. There was plenty of work
to do, and always something new coming along.[8]

Frances had done well in school, so the McClellands were not surprised to
see their son perform ably too. Through his junior year, Norman attended high
school in the Amphitheater District School on Prince Road. Then, he remembered, "during the war, due to the gasoline shortage and transportation problems, we moved to a house on East Lee Street—in what we would call 'downtown'—which involved a transfer to Tucson High for my senior year."[9]

What followed was a year of college, at the University of Arizona, plus two summer sessions, then a stint in the Air Force from August 1945 to December 1946. The fighting part of the war was over by then; after basic training in Biloxi, Mississippi, Norman joined the Army of Occupation in Weisbaden, Germany. Reenrolling in the university in January 1947, he finished his course work two and a half years later, emerging with a business degree and the bonus of having completed more than twenty units in agriculture. In 1949 he, too, joined the Shamrock Dairy.

Norman noted that his university years combined with his army experience had given him a chance to have "a good look around to see what was going on and to recognize some of the opportunities that being part of the family enterprise could offer. My mother and father complemented each other in business, and despite their differing personalities, my dad and my uncle also got along extremely well. They both spent a lot of time talking about things together and figuring out what to do. I could see myself becoming part of that good working relationship. Besides, I always thought I wanted to be like Bill Parker; it was a lot of fun just being around him."[10]

NORMAN MCCLELLAND

Like Dad, my uncle was both progressive and willing to try out new ideas and methods. He was extremely supportive of the next generation, particularly when it came to growing the company through acquisitions. He also proved a remarkable risk-taker when he came out strongly in favor of our building the processing plant in Phoenix. His part of Shamrock was on the line just as much as the McClellands', and over the years he always expressed pride in the achievements of the company and in the direction my own leadership was taking it.[11]

I started out in accounting, learning how to post sales and close the books; then as time went on I went into sales. Shortly after that, Dad and Bill Parker asked me to manage the plant. I was very fortunate in that both my father and my uncle gave me a lot of responsibility when I came with the company, and as much authority as I was capable of taking and developing. So in a comparatively few years I was given the responsibility for our plant operation, working closely with the personnel manager, Tom Stafford, who was also our sales manager.

Opportunities for expansion and growth were there for our company, and the question was whether or not we would accept those challenges and grow. It has always been a matter of having more and more opportunities for growth than we could finance. But the idea of expanding the business in those early years and then later, as Tucson really began to grow following World War II, came as much of necessity and opportunity as of anything else. If our business was to be competitive and survive, it had to grow and be equal to and as strong as any competitor in the market.[12]

As 1949 drew to a close, Shamrock began preparing for yet another enlargement of its Tucson facilities. The company's net worth that year was $651,000, and its sales volume totaled $1,807,000 from thirty-three retail and eleven wholesale routes. The first step toward expanding the facilities to accommodate far greater volume was achieved by doubling the size of the processing plant. Pasteurization and homogenization facilities would be enlarged, increasing capacity by more than 25 percent; new boilers would be installed; and an ammoniated refrigeration system would be introduced along with a new electrical system.

When the expansion was completed, milk could be processed at a rate of 1,000 gallons an hour, and with a new bottle washer and bottle filler, capacity was increased threefold—to ninety bottles a minute. Shamrock was refining its systems so it could eventually extend its reach.

Of special significance in 1949 was completion of Shamrock's quality-control laboratory. With a steam sterilizer and high heat sterilization oven, it was equipped to perform bacterial plate counts and microscopic counts according to the U.S. Standards of Milk Analysts. With this new laboratory, milk from outside producers could be analyzed for flavor and keeping quality, as well as for bacterial content. Water and washing solutions could also be analyzed, and all products packaged for sale could be strictly controlled and tested. Because of this lab, a complete program for controlling milk quality all the way from producer to customer could be created.

NORMAN MCCLELLAND

Putting in the laboratory was one of the most important things we did then. It enabled us to begin testing for quality on a regular basis for the first time. We'd never had an official laboratory before. And we started making cottage cheese shortly thereafter, even before the next phase of plant expansion, although there was barely enough room.[13]

MILT SIVESIND

Room for two cottage-cheese vats as well as cultured buttermilk allowed Shamrock to begin manufacturing products that really brought the company to the forefront. Shamrock knew how to make cottage cheese that was better than anyone else's. Because sanitation methods were adhered to strictly, the product had long keeping quality. Well-cooked but tender curd was created through careful heating, and an electronic meter was used to determine the exact time to stop cooking and drain off the whey. Sterile refrigerated water was used to cool the cheese curd prior to its being creamed and packed.

In addition, the creaming process, called cheese dressing, was carefully formulated. The dressing was separately vat pasteurized and cooled before being introduced to the cheese curd. No preservatives were added to the cheese or any other Shamrock products. However, good, healthful, and beneficial cultures—streptococcus citroversus and para citroversus—were added to the cheese dressing to enhance the flavor and keeping quality of the cottage cheese. Clearly, good scientific procedures for product handling plus sound engineering and quality equipment, good know-how and a management group that strived for the very best—always—continued to be the way of life at Shamrock.[14]

A proper place to repair delivery trucks was also badly needed, so high priority was given to building a new service garage as well as a new warehouse in 1950. That year, Shamrock Dairy joined the computer movement with the purchase of an IBM accounting computer, a keypunch, a sorter, and a "reproducer." Arrival of this new equipment marked the underpinnings of what was to become a sophisticated computer department that would make use of more and more of the rapidly advancing technology in the years to come.

Shamrock acquired its first refrigerated truck in 1951 and began hauling milk in gleaming stainless-steel tankers in 1953. Eventually there would be a fully refrigerated fleet. Electrical plug-in areas, partly roofed over, were created exclusively for the drivers' use at the dairy. That year, Norman was married for the first time, a union that produced a daughter, Katherine, and a son, William Kent McClelland.

Nineteen fifty-three saw the establishment of the Shamrock Milk Transport Company, with Bill Boyce, its manager, responsible for refining the burgeoning milk-distribution system. Like his father before him, Bill was devoted to dairy work. After many years of hauling milk to dairy plants from producers all over the Salt River Valley, he had come to know nearly all the milk-producing farmers and the trucking business as well. His wife, Florence, who had also been raised in the dairy business, worked side by side with Bill, keeping the books and helping him solve many of the daily problems that faced the fledgling company.

NORMAN MCCLELLAND

In 1955, Bill began looking for a separate location. I told him it had to be very inexpensive. The site he found was on South Seventh Street just north of the Salt River, not far from the present freeway running east and west. We paid fifty dollars a month to rent a piece of bare ground with an old building that served as our office. At that time the Transport Company consisted of four milk tankers and four leased tractor trailers; later, refrigerated vans were added to haul finished product.

I can remember that one of the milk tankers we bought didn't have a milk pump, so Bill, Adam Ibe, and Al Heath had to improvise. They put a regular plant milk pump into a pickup truck and accompanied the tanker to the producers' farms to pump milk from the farm tanks into the tanker until a real pump could be mounted permanently on that transport tanker. This typified the "can-do" attitude that prevailed everywhere at Shamrock.[15]

In 1954, the Shamrock Dairy Federal Credit Union was organized. "It was Mr. Mac's idea, and he was one of its prime movers," said routeman Dick Oxnam, who served as its first treasurer. "Mr. Mac's account was number one, and Mrs. Mac's was number two. The credit union has all the basic services of a large bank—savings, share drafts, IRA certificates, loans—and our rates are competitive with other institutions of this type. When we joined the Arizona Clearing House, we were linked with financial institutions across the country. We could wire funds back and forth in a matter of hours."[16]

Nineteen fifty-four was also the year Mr. Mac became chairman of the Shamrock Dairy and Norman was named president.

NORMAN MCCLELLAND

I really felt good about the way my father handled me. What
he did was say, "Norman, here's the business. If you want to get in
and work hard and make a success out of it and take over, I'd love
to have you do it, and I will not interfere with what you want to
do." And he never did.[17]

As Shamrock's business grew, the management group grew with it. To each
member it was clear that sustained growth could be achieved only by continuing to earn a substantial profit after taxes. Growth meant expanding market
share and developing new market areas; it also meant money needed for trucks,
plant buildings and equipment, and money to cover accounts receivable and
inventory. All these needs had to be met out of after-tax earnings. In addition,
during World War II and up until 1950, Shamrock financed a great many milk
producers to ensure a continuing and adequate milk supply, a common practice
among all major distributors in the Salt River Valley. For the company to prosper, planned growth had to become its motto, suggesting a series of established
roadways built on faultlessly solid foundations.

One of these involved its employees, the heart of the company's spirit and
a primary source of its productivity. Shamrock, through Mr. Mac and Bill
Parker, had always been fair and honest in relations with its employees. From
the beginning, there had been an atmosphere of mutual respect plus a familial
feeling but, from Norman's viewpoint, that good feeling was perennially undercut by relations with the Teamsters' Union.

NORMAN MCCLELLAND

For years, as a family member, I had witnessed the regular
two-year cycle involving our union contract renewal and how my

mother and father dealt with it. Six months prior to the contract deadline, a hate campaign against the company would be instituted by the union that would often generate some very bad feeling. As the contract deadline came near, there also came the Los Angeles union representative and meetings between dairy companies and the union until an industrywide agreement was signed.

I distinctly remember one of the first bargaining sessions I attended as a member of the management group, back in 1949 or 1950. Carnation said they were going to sign, as the contract had already been agreed to in California. But provisions in the contract that obviously benefited Carnation were contrary to the best interests of Shamrock and its employees. The realities were obvious. The larger regional and national dairies were tied to regional or national union agreements, but Shamrock could no longer oversee the future of the company and its employees properly with a union contract. I felt that as an independent company, we needed to carve out our own destiny and could do so better ourselves than through a third party.

More important, I could no longer endure that annual or biannual ritual wherein coworkers would be pitted against each other to further union demands. I resolved not to operate the company as a union company no matter what the consequences.

With growth and a strong market position have come sales volume increases that allowed Shamrock to lead the market in wage and compensation payments. We have also tried to look at both sides of the economic question where wages and working conditions are concerned—from the employees' as well as the company's viewpoint. And so the path from a commitment to operate in the best interests of the customers, the employees and the company as a whole led us to become innovative in how we should operate and compensate our Shamrock coworkers.

It was Tom Stafford who helped us tear down the walls of distrust and replace them with mutual respect and a willingness to try a new form of compensation, with the understanding and commitment on the part of Shamrock that no employee would be compromised in the process. If the new compensation plan didn't work, we would replace it with one that would, with the assurance and trust that all would benefit long term.[18]

What Shamrock devised under Norman's management was, indeed, innovative. It was a totally new distributor system, adopted in 1955 and still in existence in modified form today, through which the company eliminated its paid routemen, all of whom were offered the opportunity to buy their former retail delivery routes. Later, the wholesale routes would be sold off in a similar manner. Contracts were framed to protect both the company and the individual distributor. After all, if it was to succeed, the new system had to be beneficial to both sides, and if Shamrock's business was to continue to grow, the individual distributors as a group had to prosper.

The advantages of this new arrangement to the individual distributor were that he now had complete control of his enterprises. In short, he was in business for himself, an entrepreneur. He could choose what time of day to serve his customers, what days of the week to make deliveries and even how many customers to serve. He was responsible for soliciting customers, and they were limited in number only by however many of them he could service comfortably.

There were incentives for him to build his route to the fullest extent possible, however, and he didn't have to just deliver dairy products—some distributors added bread and bacon to their menus of portable staples— but what dairy products he did carry had to be exclusively Shamrock's. His eventual profit was based on the difference between what he paid suppliers for product and the prices he was able to collect from his customers. He could charge whatever he wished within his own company-prescribed territory, and the more customers he had, the greater the opportunity for increasing his as well as the company's profits.

NORMAN McCLELLAND

For most distributors, managing a home-delivery business was a new ball game. They had to become managers as well as entrepreneurs. Shamrock assisted them by financing part of their business assets, such as delivery truck, accounts receivable and average units. All we required was some kind of cash down payment and then insisted that each distributor maintain a credit balance with us—that is, he would have to have enough money on deposit with the company to fund his daily purchases. The system enabled salesmen to earn more money than ever before by building new volume; they were paid incentive money for each average unit sold over the previous month. Of course, by distributing a great deal more product than they had previously, they received the increased margin or difference between their cost and the selling price.

Not everyone succeeded, but those who did were among the most industrious, men who were out working while others were sitting on their porches drinking beer. By the end of the decade most of our distributors had either made it or were gone, and Shamrock had completely changed the way we managed our business.[19]

The transition from employed routemen to distributors was gradual, and in some instances it had to adapt to existing conditions. When a distributor's route became too large to be handled, for example, Shamrock stepped in and established a "stub" route that would then be operated by a company supervisor or a relief man. When the stub route became large enough, a new man would be given the opportunity to purchase it. Indeed, through various incentives, a

distributor was encouraged to build up his route and sell off a part when it
became too big.

JOHN "JOHNNY" TORRES
Retired independent routeman in Tucson

Routes were determined by the geographic area, the number of
customers within an area, and the number of purchases per customer.
I set up my credit terms by the month, biweekly, and weekly. I asked
people when they got paid and set up my accounts accordingly. I had
to collect the money after work. On my short days I got new customers by soliciting door to door.

Distributors primarily set their own credit standards. If there was
a problem, Shamrock's credit manager would get involved and determine what the payback arrangements should be. The routeman stood
all of the responsibility for each account.[20]

The role played by independent distributors in the success of Shamrock
Dairy was exemplified by men like Johnny Torres, and by Sam Scariano, who
also owned his own truck and his own route, and was under contract to purchase
his dairy supplies from Shamrock. In order to take care of his customers as
he believed they should be cared for, Sam would perform many ancillary tasks
for them. At one stop, for example, he would give two small dogs their
vitamin pills; at another, he would look into the refrigerator of an absent house-
wife, determine what she was going to cook for dinner, and then leave the
appropriate dairy products.

Another Shamrock routeman, Jerry Dalton, said that for him there was more
to being a milkman than getting up early, driving a truck, and keeping a big smile
on his face. His job came to include changing light bulbs, moving sofas, feeding
animals, and watering house plants. And Leo Paczosa, along with his wife,

created a device that could be placed in an empty milk bottle to let the milkman know exactly what the customer wanted. One end of the device was fanlike, with all the available products listed on the folds of the fan. The customer isolated the fan "blades" containing the specific product they wished to order, and dropped the whole device into an empty container for the route man to pick up.

The independent distributor's day began before dawn. By 4:00 A.M. his fully loaded truck had left the dairy to make the 110 or so stops on his route. By 1:00 A.M. he was back at the dairy, where he inventoried his stock and reloaded his refrigerated truck with the next day's milk. Then he plugged his cooling apparatus into one of the outside electrical outlets so the system could be recharged, and for the next half-hour he attended to bookkeeping duties. By 2:30 P.M., he was heading home. And at the end of the day he could pause and reflect that, because he liked people and believed in giving service as well as delivering food products, he had achieved a satisfying life.

Chapter Six

Acquisitions and Ice Cream

By 1950, Shamrock Dairy had fulfilled most of its goals in the Tucson area, having achieved almost complete sales coverage within the city and its environs. Gradually, the sales force had begun to move into suburban areas—and to such an extent, ultimately, that it became necessary to name a supervisor of routes for the entire region, a job that fell to John Harty.

Until then John had been responsible for developing business north of Tucson where much residential development was taking place, especially along Oracle Road. Now he was venturing outside the Tucson vicinity, into communities where some Shamrock penetration had already been made but a more aggressive attitude was needed. So he went into Benson, Bisbee, and Douglas in Cochise County, into Nogales in Santa Cruz County, then north to San Manuel in Pinal County. His mandate was to expand Shamrock operations, specifically market share, which he was able to do by working with employees and distributors alike, pressing for greater sales of more and more products.

Because of his success in growing the business in southern Arizona, John Harty was the logical man to spearhead the next Shamrock move—into central Arizona. In 1954 the company decided the time had come to establish the first retail routes in Phoenix and begin competing head to head with the formidable array of dairies that existed in the fast-growing capital city. From their small base on South Seventh Street, Shamrock routemen loaded trucks, solicited home deliveries, and checked route books. Once a foothold had been established, the sales force went to work and, little by little, began expanding their customer base.

"Our entry into the Phoenix market did not go unnoticed; our competitors enlisted the union to stop or slow our growth," Norman recalled. "The Teamsters hired men to follow our Phoenix home-delivery trucks; our customers were contacted and urged not to deal with any nonunion organization. The union was successful to some extent, but we kept going and gradually added volume."[1]

Helen Hallberg Coates, who had gone to work in accounts receivable at the Tucson plant in 1952, was asked to head Shamrock's new Phoenix office. In the beginning she found that even though she "did all the dusting and cleaned the rest rooms," she still had time to "read and do a lot of embroidery work."[2] This did not last long, however. Soon a ten-acre parcel of land was acquired; expert advice was solicited, received, and processed from around the country; and by late 1955 the new Phoenix plant was under construction. It would be an ultramodern facility outfitted with a full range of mostly new equipment, enabling Shamrock to produce cottage cheese, buttermilk, and other cultured products, as well as process milk and cream. There would be an even more efficient quality-control laboratory than Shamrock had created in Tucson, plus the capability of packaging milk in both paper cartons and glass containers.

Dave Hall was at Norman's side when ground was broken for the Phoenix plant. Dave joined Shamrock in October 1955 and was directed to acquaint himself with the entire dairy operation, especially the accounting side. Ultimately he became part of Shamrock's advance guard in Phoenix, helping to expand the business so it was reasonable to expect that sufficient potential volume existed to support the kind of operation being built there.

Determined but naive, Dave, along with John Harty and Norman himself, was bursting with youthful determination. Each was prepared to work as hard as he had to for Shamrock to gain a share of the success that Borden, Carnation,

Meadow Gold, and Arden, among others, had already captured. After all, hadn't Shamrock's industry and business savvy paid off handsomely in Tucson and southern Arizona? Why wouldn't the company also triumph in Phoenix?

As the Phoenix staff began settling into its new quarters, it was clear that not all aspects of the brand-new facility had reached a full state of readiness. Much of the furniture had yet to be delivered, or even ordered, leaving unusable empty spaces that gave a decidedly tentative tone to the operation. "I was lost the first day," said Helen Coates of the shift from South Seventh Street to North Black Canyon. "Over the weekend, the men had moved my office, and my work was scattered among three desks in the office and the check-in room."[3]

At one point during Shamrock's first few days in the new facility, D. V. Welsh of the Borden Company called on Norman. As his office had not been completed, Norman was forced to receive his guest sitting on the new front steps, which hardly mattered to Norman but added to Welsh's certainty that within a few months, and "for a song," he might be able to replace his own out-moded facility with this brand-new one.

Lack of office furniture would not have bothered Tom Stafford either, had he not been swamped with job applicants needing to be interviewed. All he had at his disposal was a folding card table and some folding chairs, hardly an appropriate ambience in which to impress prospective employees. Finally, after suffering such embarrassment for several days, Tom cornered Norman at a management lunch and asked if it might be possible for him to have a suitable table for interviewing. Innocently, Norman asked what was wrong with the card table he had been using, and it was Dave Hall who answered: "The drawers stick."[4] There was laughter all around, and Tom got the furniture he needed.

How did Shamrock manage to succeed so convincingly in an arena where the competition was so overwhelming? Norman attributed the achievement simply to everyone's willingness to work very hard plus the fact that Bill Parker, along with Assistant General Manager Charles Lacy, very effectively managed the Tucson facility while the Phoenix operation was being established. But others recalled that it was Norman's collegial and supportive management style that deserved much of the credit. Shamrock's success, said Dave Hall, was "something we took for granted. We didn't necessarily do everything right, but because we worked hard, we succeeded. We did a lot of things by instinct as opposed to planning."[5]

While the Phoenix plant was still in its design phase, a relationship was developing between the dairy industry and the federal government with the issuance of an order under the Milk Market Administration System of the U. S. Department of Agriculture. The need for such an order grew out of conditions that had evolved over a period of more than twenty-five years. In the 1930s, during the Great Depression, members of the U. S. Congress had decided that a price floor should be provided under farm products, including milk, cheeses, milk powder, and other dairy products.

Congress also believed that if the federal government was to be involved, there should be a strict accounting of milk received by handlers (those who bottled the milk) as well as an accounting of milk furnished by producers (the dairy farmers), both as to pounds of fluid and of butterfat. Butterfat tests, in particular, would be monitored carefully, as such tests, in part, would establish the basis for payment.

Shamrock was just one of a large number of milk-product distributors in the Phoenix area, all of whom bought from local producers at rates based on pounds of milk and butterfat. At Shamrock the federal order was not viewed negatively, as it would require all handlers to account totally for the product they received and pay the same price for their milk. Norman, for one, felt that Shamrock would be more comfortable with the assurance that all producers and all distributors were being treated equally. It had been Shamrock's policy to pay a premium of three or four cents for each pound of butterfat in order to obtain the highest quality milk, so the Central Arizona Milk Marketing Order did not make any great change in the way Shamrock operated.

Another long-standing policy, established in 1953, had been for Shamrock to use its own tankers to pick up milk from farmers and then ascertain its quality right at the platform of its processing plants before pumping the milk into storage. "To this day we screen out milk that does not meet our standards, never actually absorbing it into our plants," said Norman.[6] Clearly, quality had been an important consideration at Shamrock long before the federal order was even drafted, and it remained so thereafter. Shamrock Dairy maintained its own staff in the field and in the transport system to ensure the uniform excellence of its product.

Despite the concentration of effort in Phoenix and the Salt River Valley between 1954 and 1956, Shamrock people were not letting any opportunities elsewhere escape them, particularly in southern and southwestern Arizona. Although its dairy products were already being marketed in Cochise County, Shamrock completed arrangements to purchase Cloverleaf Dairy in 1955, thus creating a strong impetus to capture the bulk of the dairy business in Bisbee, Cochise County's most populous community. Shamrock's Tucson-based sales force kept up its aggressive campaigns elsewhere, all across the lower third of Arizona, to see that Shamrock product sales were leading those of its competitors.

After the big push to Phoenix in 1956, which created an immediate surge in Shamrock business throughout central Arizona, the company began to look toward Yuma in the southwest corner of the state. For two years, Shamrock had been buying milk from dairy farmers in Yuma County in exchange for their consideration.

NORMAN McCLELLAND

The creameries to which they had been shipping could only use part of their milk, and the price for surplus milk that these producers received was consistently low. Outbidding these creameries, we began to haul tanker milk from Yuma to our Tucson plant and back-haul finished dairy products from our plant to greater Yuma. It was at about this time that we began selling dairy products in Gila Bend and Ajo from our Tucson plant through Malin Lewis Distributing. We were anxious to develop these markets ourselves, as we had determined that product earmarked for them would be processed at our Phoenix facility.[7]

In March 1958, negotiations were completed for Shamrock to purchase Jersey Farms Dairy in Yuma, thereby gaining a valuable satellite that served the entire Yuma Valley plus key points in California, just across the Colorado River. At about this time Shamrock bought out Malin Lewis's business in Yuma. "It seemed that the timing was right for Malin to sell his Yuma distributorship to Shamrock," Dave Hall noted.[8]

These two acquisitions gave the company a strong foothold in Yuma. As they were brought into the Shamrock system, other opportunities presented themselves. In May 1959, Desert Gold Dairy of Casa Grande, located about halfway between Tucson and Phoenix, became available for purchase. A few months later, Purity Dairy of Douglas, in Cochise County, was added, creating a new source of business near the Mexican border.

For a brief period after Jersey Farms Dairy was acquired, its label was retained to provide continuity with the customers. Shamrock made its company identity known, however, as supervisors invested a greater-than-ever effort to respond to customer needs and maintain a high level of service so that the new Shamrock brand would ultimately be welcomed.

Shamrock made its strongest push into Yuma in 1960 by purchasing Sunland Dairy, which not only processed milk but also had the capacity to manufacture ice cream on a limited basis. This brought a three-label situation into the picture; for a time the Sunland label continued to appear alongside that of Jersey Farms and of Shamrock itself. Gradually, the local brand names were discontinued as Shamrock solidified a commanding position in the community, using its delivery equipment as mobile billboards to familiarize area residents with all of its dairy products.

Soon after purchasing Sunland Dairy, Shamrock began shipping it truckloads of bottled milk from Phoenix to distribute in Yuma, and Sunland itself was converted into one large ice cream plant that would eventually manufacture enough product on a full-time basis to supply customers statewide. But the biggest change in Yuma, from Shamrock's standpoint, was a stepped-up sales effort. With ice cream production rising, the salesmen waged an aggressive campaign that began with offers to rent ice cream cabinets to wholesale customers throughout the area. The renting process was predictably transitional, for as the ice cream business grew, the emphasis gradually shifted to actual cabinet sales.

By 1961, Shamrock was pressing for growth in and around Casa Grande, where it had purchased Desert Gold Dairy from Sam Parks two years earlier. Now Shamrock people were intent on promoting the company name and image throughout Pinal County. It was also from Casa Grande that countywide ice cream distribution occurred. Shamrock had built a loading dock with a milk cold room, a freezer room, an office and truck parking facilities in Casa Grande shortly after acquiring Desert Gold. Sam Parks remained with the company until he was ready to retire, serving as an adviser to Shamrock in Casa Grande.

In October 1961, Shamrock purchased the dairy distribution business of James Cooper in the town of Coolidge, not far from Casa Grande, and a large cold room with individual load-out doors was added to Shamrock's distribution facility in Tucson. Three years later, Prescott Farms Dairy was acquired. Located in Prescott, the heart of Arizona, the dairy was owned and operated by Kenny Crow and Jim Willis. After the purchase, Shamrock products were brought in and Jim was retained as the company manager for the Prescott area.

Prescott Farms Dairy was a key acquisition for Shamrock because it distributed products in northern Arizona—in Chino Valley, Ash Fork, Williams, and Flagstaff as well as Prescott. Dave Hall remembered driving up with Norman to look over the facility. The asking price for Prescott Farms was $300,000, but by Norman's seat-of-the-pants assessment the herd alone was worth $300,000— or more. In good conscience he felt he could not simply write out a check and make a deal.

Dave Hall

We had planned to stay overnight in Prescott, so we went back to the motel to talk about it. We could see that the partners were good, hardworking guys. We also recognized that they had no idea of the value of their business. Norman said, "Well, we can't just take advantage of them." After some discussion, we decided that instead of making a bid, we would offer advice.

We met for breakfast the next morning. I don't recall Norman's exact words, but I have a clear recollection of his saying that before we did anything further, it would be wise for Crow and Willis to consult a good CPA and a lawyer, because their asking price was not even close to what the company was worth. Norman might even have said, "We think the cattle alone are worth over $300,000." At any rate, they took our advice, and we eventually worked it out. One fellow kept the cattle, and the other fellow went to work for us. At the time it didn't seem like a big deal; it was just playing fair—and being honest.[9]

In 1965, the retail distribution of Sweet Milk Dairy in Phoenix was acquired along with Roosevelt Dairy in nearby Mesa, both of which added volume to the milk available to Shamrock and supplemented the territory already being served in the Salt River Valley. By that time, Dave Hall recalled, "I think we had attained better than thirty percent of the total dairy volume in Arizona. All of our acquisitions were designed to put us in areas where we'd had no presence."[10]

Acquiring Sunland Dairy turned out to be Shamrock's most significant move in the early sixties. The building itself had been started before the turn of the twentieth century. It was to have been a church, but parishioners had run out of funds after completing a large concrete-walled basement. The structure that was finally erected would be home to a Prohibition-era speakeasy until it became the Challenge Cream and Butter Company, then after an ownership change, the

Yuma Creamery. It was under Aux Ambort, a Swiss immigrant, that the name Sunland Dairy was born.

In making this acquisition, Shamrock would profit not only because of the plant it had bought but also because of the talent and reputation of the man they had bought it from: its current chief executive, Chad Cox. A Utah State University graduate who had developed a peerless talent for making ice cream, he had acquired a controlling interest in Sunland from Aux Ambort.

CHAD COX
Former owner of Sunland Dairy and Shamrock's original
ice cream plant manager

In March 1940, Mr. Ambort expanded his Sunland operation to include Yuma, through purchase of the Yuma Creamery from Fred Teller. A few months later, I came there to supervise the Sunland plant. After a couple of years I was made manager of the operation, then shortly thereafter Mr. Ambort and I formed a partnership. A few years later, we incorporated and I took control as president and general manager.

In 1960, Norman McClelland and Dave Hall contacted me about selling Sunland Dairy to Shamrock. After a few weeks of negotiations, we settled on a merger date, and at that time Shamrock Dairy took over all of the assets of Sunland Dairy and made plans to convert the plant to a straight ice cream operation. We were slow getting everything set up the way we needed to in the way of ice cream storage and transportation, but there was progress continuously in that direction. We had full cooperation in increasing our capacity in Yuma by purchasing better equipment and adopting better techniques for handling product.

To this end we obtained advice regularly from some of the best people in the field, including Dr. Chester Dahl, a highly regarded consultant from Penn State University. I was impressed with Professor Dahl and his work, having read his textbooks while studying dairy manufacturing, my college major. He was very progressive, and a big help to us in getting things set up properly.[11]

Shamrock's immediate challenge was to make Sunland's ice cream manufacturing plant the source of enough product to supply the growing statewide demand. Until then Shamrock had not been a serious contender in the ice cream arena. After ending its short-lived ownership of Frozenpure Ice Cream in 1942, the company had merely dabbled in the distribution of ice cream and ice cream novelties—packaged cones, bars and sandwiches—all of which had been obtained from Golden State, which eventually became Foremost Dairy.

As early as 1948, Mr. Mac had expressed the wish that ice cream be part of the Shamrock product line once more, but the timing was not propitious. In the immediate postwar years, Shamrock was growing so rapidly that just getting its existing product to its targeted new markets was a formidable challenge. A dozen years passed before the company would be able to focus on acquiring an ice cream facility of its own or to seek out a source of ice cream for which it would become the distribution agent. In 1960, when Sunland Dairy and the Cox ice cream manufacturing plant became part of Shamrock, Mr. Mac's dream was finally realized.

A year later, when quantity processing of ice cream began in earnest, the hauling of ice cream to Phoenix and Tucson got under way. Increased production justified the decision to send Shamrock Transport Company's tankers from Phoenix to Yuma filled with the grade-A milk and cream with which to make the ice cream mix. Those same tankers hauled grade-A raw milk produced in the Yuma area back to the milk plant in Phoenix, and Transport Company vehicles also carried bulk ice cream and novelties from Yuma to distribution points in Tucson and Phoenix.

A number of Sunland Dairy's employees had remained with the company after it was sold, helping the Shamrock staff become fully acquainted with this important new arm of their dairy operation. Additionally, Dave Hall and Bill Boyce of Shamrock and Art Kossak of Sunland traveled east to take special courses at Pennsylvania State University to further their education in the way to manage and operate a profitable ice cream business.

Chad Cox was among those who stayed on after the transfer of ownership, and his continued association with the company was mutually beneficial. Shamrock furnished the necessary resources for an expanded operation, and Chad furnished the knowledge and experience that would foment the development of quality ice cream not only to draw business from competitors but also to develop ice cream outlets that had never been served before. As production increased, ice cream was offered to the public under such names as Sun Dipt Ice Milk, Erin Gold Ice Cream, and Emerald Isle, plus Sweet Surprise, which was an imitation ice milk product.

Joe Williams, who worked both in and outside the Sunland plant for seventeen years before its purchase by Shamrock, recalled a production gaffe that ultimately surfaced as an ice cream innovation.

JOSEPH "JOE" WILLIAMS
Former Sunland and Shamrock ice cream employee

I really goofed one day while making a batch of vanilla ice cream for the Eskimo Pie Ice Cream Bars in the batch freezer. I noticed that the chocolate bar coating tank was too full, so I took out sixteen to twenty ounces with a stainless-steel beaker and placed it next to the freezer. Now when it came time to flavor the batch with the vanilla extract, I poured the chocolate coating into the ice cream instead, and the dasher quickly mixed it all together.

I ran to the office right away and told Chad Cox that I'd ruined ten gallons of ice cream and described how I had done it. He said,

"Well, go ahead and put the vanilla in it anyway, finish freezing the batch and put it in some bulk cans." After doing this I told Chad the ice cream tasted good, though it looked funny with little chocolate flakes all through it. Chad phoned the owner of Frank's Pharmacy in downtown Yuma, as they had a soda fountain, and offered a discount price if he would sell this ice cream in cones. Chad called the ice cream Chocolate Flake, when talking to the drugstore owner, but at the dairy we all called it Joe's Boo Boo.

To my surprise, it sold very well and when the soda fountain ran out, the owner told his route salesman that more was needed. In response, I said I had made one mistake and didn't intend to make another one. Can you imagine how funny I felt a few years later when I saw practically the same product hit the market labeled Chocolate Chip?[12]

After taking over the Sunland plant, Shamrock set about remodeling it, building an addition to the cold-storage facility and installing a modern two-stage, low-temperature ammoniated refrigeration system. An additional 400-gallon-per-hour ice cream continuous freezer was obtained along with fruit-feeder-flavoring equipment and packaging machinery.

CHAD COX

We soon had a reputation for making the best possible use of the space available and getting the greatest possible gallonage per man-hour of production time. We maximized the facilities we had and continually budgeted to improve our processing and hardening capacity to meet demands of the sales department for product. By 1977 we were able to raise our total production to between two and three million gallons a year. We met our initial goal within a year, manufacturing and selling up to 30,000 gallons of ice cream a month. Twenty years later we were turning out that much in just two days.[13]

MILT SIVESIND

From the very outset of our venture into ice cream manufacture, it was Shamrock's goal to have the very best product available in our market area. On November 15 and 16, 1960, Dr. Dahl joined Chad Cox and me to conduct a flavoring and tasting panel to evaluate our products along with all other brands of ice cream in our market area—from Borden's, Carnation, Arden, Swift, Golden State, and Safeway.

The only ice cream that beat ours was Safeway's, and that was because we still had old freezers and the body, texture, and iciness of our product was not smooth, like Safeway's. Shamrock set out to correct the problems by bringing in the best equipment engineered to freeze and harden the product.

In May 1961, Dr. Dahl returned for three days to counsel us further in ways to improve the operation of our ice cream plant and, in addition, to be involved in another flavoring and tasting test of product. Ten different flavors and six brand names, including Shamrock's, were judged and evaluated. We felt we had a nice, clean, good-flavored product, but we listened to all the recommendations. What we learned was that we needed to distribute fruit and nuts more evenly in the ice cream; we needed a new machine to fill cartons; we needed more warehouse space; we needed vats for storing and flavoring; we needed to pasteurize the ice cream mix better and more efficiently; but mostly we needed more refrigeration and *colder* refrigeration for the ice cream freezer and for quickly cooling the freshly filled product to twenty below zero.

Within a year of the May 1961 meeting, nearly all of these needs had been answered, but Dr. Dahl continued to help us at least the first seven years of starting in the ice cream business. Our goal was to manufacture the best product on the market, so it followed that larger and larger volume was called for.[14]

Joe Williams remembered that the first Shamrock ice cream account in the Salt River Valley to be served from the Yuma plant was a new 7-Eleven store in Chandler. Because the ice cream handling facilities in Phoenix would not be on line until June 1961, Chandler had to be supplied with ice cream that had been delivered to Casa Grande from Yuma. But when the Phoenix operation began, other 7-Eleven stores in the Salt River Valley became customers. One truck, packed only with ice cream products, was assigned the deliveries.

JOE WILLIAMS

Small grocery stores, drugstores, and restaurants were good business targets for us in the 1960s. We sometimes called them bread-and-butter accounts, as we were building a good business working with these customers and it was profitable to serve them. Shamrock Dairy's rapid growth was obtained through these many accounts and retail routes throughout the area.

After surveying metropolitan Phoenix, I concluded that the potential for selling ice cream was enormous, that many of our potential customers were receiving poor service and that our competitors didn't seem to have product knowledge or to understand customer flavor preference. I even overheard the general manager of the largest processor of dairy products and ice cream products in the state stand up and tell a group that the people of Arizona didn't want a premium- or even a good-quality ice cream—"all they want is something cold, sweet, and *cheap*, and this is what we give them." I was determined to prove this was a false statement.[15]

Shamrock's ice cream promotion people went into elaborate detail in planning and outlining its sales campaign. They drew up "plan-o-grams" for different types of outlets—supermarkets, grocery stores, convenience stores— and even for different-size display cabinets. Routemen were hired with no ice cream experience so that Shamrock could train them in its own methods and sales approach. Classes were conducted to give these men product knowledge, to familiarize them with the ingredients and the ice cream manufacturing process. In some supermarkets, Shamrock product had more than one competitor, so supervisors worked to obtain the best location in each store for the freezer cases. In some of the biggest stores, demonstrators were on hand to distribute Shamrock samples to the public.

When sales outpaced production at the Yuma plant, Shamrock enriched its supply of ice cream by acquiring Bratt Ice Cream Company, which added about $60,000 a month to the sales volume. Swift Ice Cream Company was going out of business about the time Shamrock was beginning to surge ahead, and some of that volume was captured by Shamrock's sales force. Arden Company sold out to Carnation, thereby eliminating a major ice cream producer.

Sales and production soon balanced out, and the plant was producing what was needed to fill the demand. During its first year in operation, the Yuma plant manufactured 200,000 gallons of ice cream. A dozen years later a new central ice cream warehouse was completed in Phoenix, with five times the storage capacity of its predecessor. Because it was designed to serve the entire state, ice cream and frozen desserts manufactured in Yuma were transported under minus-twenty-degree temperature to Phoenix.

Additional acquisitions facilitated much of the growth, but in buying Bratt's in Phoenix, Roosevelt Dairy in Mesa, and New Modern Dairy serving the Globe-Miami area, Shamrock not only increased market share but productivity as well. Shipped to the Yuma plant were vats and tanks that tripled the gallonage capacity, a boiler, an ammonia compressor, a pasteurizing system, a homogenizer, a cooling tower and an ice builder for plant-cooling water and vats. It was Gilbert Wheeler, Shamrock's new ice cream plant foreman, who automated the cleaning and container systems. According to Milt Sivesind, "Cartons began to be manufactured on the spot, then immediately filled and frozen in multiple lines of production."[16]

The mid-1970s saw ice cream manufacturing at Shamrock's Yuma plant reach even higher degrees of efficiency and sophistication. The mix was pasteurized and homogenized so that the ice cream would be smoother and creamier. Ingredients were carefully measured and pumped into the mixer. After the flavor and fruit or nuts were added, the mix went through the freezer where it became the finished product.

While the freezer was making the ice cream—from a combination of milk, cream, sugar and natural flavors—another machine was forming the round half-gallon cartons, which were then dispatched by conveyor to the filler and packaging machine. There, each carton was filled, capped and sealed. No hands touched the product until the customer actually opened the carton.

Ice cream was also packed in square half-gallon cartons filled the same way. These were sent by conveyor belt to the cold room for hardening; they were stored there for twenty-four hours at a temperature at least twenty-five degrees below zero. Ice cream cartons were placed in racks and loaded on large refrigerated vans at temperatures kept at twenty below zero. The vans transported the product to cold-storage rooms at the various Shamrock distributing centers throughout Arizona.

By 1977, Shamrock was producing and packing ice cream for such large supermarket chains as Bashas', Smitty's, and Fry's, whose own labels were stamped on the cartons. In addition, Shamrock's own sales plus private-label product volume had exceeded 100,000 gallons of ice cream a month, which was supplied to its Arizona customers.

There was no single element that contributed to the success of Shamrock ice cream, no magic formula or fortuitous event. What "secret" existed was revealed years later in a modestly worded statement by Milt Sivesind: "Efficiency and product quality were reflected in the quality of our personnel."[17]

Chapter Seven

Following the Herd

$\mathcal{T}$he first edition of the *Shamrock News* carried this special salute to the Guernsey cattle of Shamrock Dairy:

> If you had lived on this continent prior to the European invasion of the 17th century, your diet would have included sheep, goat or mare's milk. You would have waited until Columbus arrived on his second voyage here in order to enjoy cows' milk. The familiar fawn and white Guernsey was brought to Boston by a pirate whose ship had been wrecked on the island of Guernsey located in the English Channel. Captain Prince found the cattle there not only beautiful but also producers of a fine, creamy milk with a delicious flavor.
>
> From the very beginning of Shamrock Dairy, the Shamrock registered Guernsey herd has played an integral part in their milk program with Golden Guernsey milk products. [In 1932] Mr. Mac purchased his first registered Guernsey and in 1935 registered his first animal bred by him....Mr. Mac traveled far and wide to select the correct bloodlines for the improvement of his herd and breed.... The purpose was to bring into the herd new blood to fuse with the fountainhead of established Shamrock bloodlines.[1]

In the early years of Shamrock, the herd was kept at what became known as the Guernsey Farm, located on the site of the dairy's original milking and processing facility in Tucson. The farm was actually a twenty-four cow flat barn that stood across a road from the processing plant to which milk, in giant cans, had to be hand carried. The Shamrock herd gradually grew in size from periodic infusions of new blood. In 1934, a purebred Guernsey bull, Foremost Royal Bell Buoy, was brought to Shamrock from the J. C. Penney farm in New York State, and ten select Guernsey cows were moved in from Idaho. Before the end of the decade, there would be close to sixty animals at the Guernsey Farm.

As the herd grew, the facilities frequently had to be enlarged. Shamrock itself produced most of the animals that were added to its milk-producing herd, and by using the best available bulls, was able to keep improving the quality and productivity of its herd. The need for more milk ultimately outdistanced herd size, however, although more than 250 cows were being milked daily at the Guernsey Farm by 1959 and a new milking parlor was built to accommodate them. Shamrock grew increasingly dependent on outside producers to keep up with the swelling demand for milk in the region.

Tucson's remarkable growth helped grow the business; it also began to create problems for Shamrock Dairy and the Guernsey Farm, which had been considered out-of-town facilities at the time they were established. But as subdivision after subdivision was developed, the presence of a dairy and its animals came to be something less than desirable in a community that was filling in the open spaces and becoming a virtual city.

"Our primary milking herd was literally up the street from the dairy processing plant in Tucson," wrote office manager Ted Springer in 1983. "It eventually became overpopulated, and although legally the McClellands did not have to move the herd, they did so [in 1965] for the benefit of the community, moving...to a new farm on Cortaro Farms Road. The McClellands donated nine acres of farmland to the Flowing Wells School District, and with some county land it became the McClelland Educational Park adjoining the Flowing Wells Junior High School."[2]

With the capacity for milking 1,000 cows daily, the Cortaro plant, located some fourteen miles northwest of Tucson, incorporated many of the currently most innovative ideas about dairying and milk production. To keep sales well ahead of production, Shamrock Dairy launched an advertising campaign that would stoke the popularity of its Guernsey Royal milk. Produced from Guernseys only, it was rich in color—the result of its well above average cream content—and high in nonfat solids.

Meanwhile, to continually upgrade their Guernsey herd, the McClellands were acquiring the offspring of prizewinning bulls. They were aided in this particular quest by an important development in the 1960s. At that time the U. S. Department of Agriculture had begun producing computerized information by which the owner of a dairy bull could classify his animal by type and milk production. This made it possible to select bulls with the greatest promise of producing improved milk cows—bulls that, through artificial insemination, could become the sires of dozens of calves in a great many herds.

In 1962, a two-year-old Guernsey heifer was among the feature attractions at Shamrock's fortieth anniversary celebration. Daisy's Dawn of Les Beauchamp, a registered Guernsey from the Isle of Guernsey, had been purchased by the McClellands while touring the island that year in search of possible herd additions. Guernsey milk being high in both color and fat content, its demand rose as Arizona's population expanded. This high demand increased the number of Guernsey breeders in the state, and Mr. Mac was certainly one of the most active among them. He had been instrumental in organizing the Arizona Guernsey Cattle Club back in 1929, though he did not serve as one of its original officers.

Interest in breeding Guernsey cattle and selling their milk led Mr. Mac to join an organization known as Golden Guernsey, Inc., in May 1950. This affiliation gave him license to use the name Golden Guernsey in marketing and selling Shamrock products from Guernsey cows. Each year the organization issued a report on the major achievements of its members, including the amount of Guernsey milk sold. It took time, but Shamrock finally did join the upper ranks of national Guernsey-product sellers: In 1958, it was number eleven in the country; in the early '60s, for four years straight, it was number four before finally achieving the number two spot in 1970.

The trend toward selling directly to wholesalers rather than to retail customers at home gradually reduced the importance of identifying the end product as milk from any one breed of cow. Another trend—toward establishing fewer but larger milk plants—made it increasingly difficult to keep Guernsey milk separate in processing plants or even at the producer milk pickup stage. In addition, by 1970 Shamrock was packaging milk under private labels, and the volume created by this and other marketing innovations made the Golden Guernsey label gradually less important to sales. Even so, the company continued to sustain a strong Guernsey program, with separate milk pickup and processing, and also continued to market products under the Golden Guernsey label. A premium over the federal order was also paid to producers to encourage an ongoing supply of Guernsey product.

Despite the diminishing importance of Guernsey milk from a marketing standpoint, some important new production records were established by Shamrock Guernseys during the early '70s. In September 1970, for example, Shamrock learned that its Neslekcim Fortune Daisy, whose output totaled 27,990 pounds of milk in 365 days, had become the highest official Guernsey record holder for milk production to date. She was just under four years old, and her record-setting production averaged 91.44 pounds per day. Purchased by Shamrock along with several of her paternal sisters, this outstanding cow had been bred by George Mickelsen of Petaluma, California ("Neslekcim" being "Mickelsen" spelled backward).

Less than a year later, another of Shamrock's registered Guernsey cows, Diversified Buster Ivory, a four-year-old bred by Walter Matthiesen of Filer, Idaho, set a new record by producing 725 pounds of fat and 21,110 pounds of milk in 305 days of twice-daily milking. She was fifth among the ten highest producers of the Guernsey breed in her class, nationally.

Early the following year, Norman was notified that Shamrock was to receive two Golden Guernsey Awards for 1971. The first recognized

Shamrock's having become the second largest distributor in the nation for the second time; the other award acknowledged that Shamrock's Guernsey milk output had achieved the second largest quart increase during the year.

The Shamrock herd's next move resulted not only from the company's desire to consolidate its cattle holdings but also from some deft estate planning on Norman's part when it became clear that Bill Parker's son, James, had a dedicated interest in dairying. "[James Parker] has worked in every area of the farm operation," Norman wrote when announcing Jim's promotion in 1980. "He started with the Shamrock Farms Company in December 1976 as a management trainee. In June 1978 he was promoted to the position of manager, Chandler Farms. [Now] as assistant general manager, Jim will report to the general manager, Shamrock Farms Company, and will assist him in all areas of the total farm operation."[3]

Aware that Jim was an outdoorsman, more at home in faded jeans than in business suits, Frances McClelland suggested encouraging Jim to become involved in farm management.

FRANCES MCCLELLAND

And so Jim got into the farm business and took to it very well. Eventually we came to a point where the Parkers and the McClellands split their interest so they could do their thing and we could do ours....At that point, Bill Parker was still involved, although somewhat retired. We put all the farms, the foods company, and the dairy together in a partnership, and then a few years later the Parkers took their interest out all in Parker Dairy Farms and we took our interest out all in Shamrock Foods, but there was one farm left over, the Shamrock Hill Farm on Contaro Farms Road, which we kept.... This division gave the Parkers a chance to run their business the way they wanted to run it, not the way Norman said it had to be run.[4]

The farm designated for Jim Parker was to be built in Chandler Heights, a few miles from Shamrock's old Emerald Farm, about a thirty-minute drive south of Phoenix. Ultimately all the animals would be moved from Chandler to Chandler Heights, leaving behind an empty facility. Writing in the *Shamrock News*, Jim enthusiastically described his new domain.

JAMES WILLIAM "JIM" PARKER
Son of executive William Parker and co-owner of Parker Dairy Farm

We finally moved into our new farm at Chandler Heights after four years of planning and eleven months of construction. The total property covers 300 acres with 80 acres in use. We started moving cattle to this location the first of January [1983]....The distance between the two farms is about eight miles, and we made the move in four days. We first moved over the lowest producing cows, which is about half of the herd, and then the rest about four days later. We did this so that in case of any equipment problems we would not miss any milkings on the whole herd. As it turned out, the move was fairly smooth and none of the cattle got off schedule.... The amount of milk we are shipping has gone from about 50,000 pounds per day when we first moved in to about 77,000 pounds per day, and we are now milking 1,520 cows.[5]

Frances described what was to happen next.

FRANCES MCCLELLAND

It was not long before Jim began saying how much he would really like to go up to Wickenburg, which is about two hours north of

95

Phoenix. Summers in the Phoenix area are as brutal for animals as for the people who live there, and Wickenburg is much cooler. So we said, OK, we'll build you a farm in Wickenburg and we'll trade for the Chandler Heights farm. And that's what we did.

To build a whole operation like that takes money, but by that point we were eager to close down the farm in Tucson. The Hill Farm had become surrounded by housing developments, and even though we had been there first, we were getting complaints about the smell. So we built the Wickenburg farm for Jim and moved out of Tucson into Chandler Heights.

We didn't expand Chandler Heights at the time we moved. But shortly thereafter Norman discovered an innovative system that allowed a lot more cows to be milked for the same amount of money. And so, in 1991, both milking barns were remodeled and we pretty much doubled our herd size, milking close to 6,000 cows twice a day.[6]

In 1989 Jim reported in the *Shamrock News* on the progress of the new Parker Dairy Farm, built on 800 acres of previously undeveloped desert at the foot of Weaver Mountains, nineteen miles northeast of Wickenburg.

JIM PARKER

Temperatures are 10 to 15 degrees cooler than the Phoenix area, and that is the primary reason for choosing this location....We will be milking 3,000 cows within six months of opening up, from our current 2,500 cows....We raise all of our female heifer calves for replacement stock, so total animals on the farm will be about 7,000....

All of our milk will be shipped to the plant in Phoenix, and I would be remiss not to mention our thanks to the Shamrock family. Bill Boyce, Bob Whitehurst, Cliff Knight, [herdsman] Jay Edgmon,

Norm McClelland, Milt Sivesind, Bob Gromko, Mr. Mac and, of course, Mr. Parker have all contributed many lifetimes' worth of knowledge, experience, and expertise to the evolution of my career as a dairyman and to the evolution of this state-of-the-art, first-class dairy farm. The Parker family hopes that all of the Shamrock family will share our pride in this facility.[7]

Milking cows and processing milk have been refined through technological achievement, but the cycle that begins with the birth of a calf and ends with her becoming a functional milking cow follows a fairly predictable, ongoing cycle. Susie Upson, who joined Shamrock Emerald Farm as a calf feeder/manager in 1980, described that cycle in articles she wrote for the *Shamrock News*.

SUSIE UPSON
Former Shamrock Farms employee

When a calf is born, it is left with its mother for anywhere from 12 to 24 hours. This gives the cow time to clean and care for the calf. It also gives the calf time to get colostrum, or first milk, from the cow. The first milk is of utmost importance to the calf's future well-being, as it is high in immune proteins which help the calf fight infection and disease. The calf is then taken from the mother and put in an individual pen. Its navel is dipped in iodine to dry it up and prevent navel infection. Because of the importance of colostrum, we offer it to the calf from a bottle to ensure it has received the colostrum. The bull, or male, calves are sold within the first few days after birth. The heifers, or females, are kept to be raised and eventually put back into the milking herd....Once the heifer is comfortably installed in her pen filled with fresh straw, her life as an integral part of dairy farming has begun. Her value in later life is based on her health, and for this reason a close watch of her eating habits, cleanliness of her pen, and her general health is maintained. The calves are fed fresh milk twice a day. This milk is from cows that have just freshened, or given birth....The calves are nursed from a bottle for the first two or three feedings, then taught to drink from a bucket. Some calves adapt to bucket feeding readily, while others seem to take forever. I imagine it is a bit like teaching a child to drink from a cup! The heifer's life is fairly routine for the first few weeks. Once she is drinking milk well, she is introduced to grain. This she nibbles in boredom at first, then attacks with gusto as her appetite increases. A lot of time is spent sleeping, but with bursts of energy she'll bounce and play in her pen, bawling loudly. There is nothing more rewarding than seeing calves playing, eyes bright and ears alert. It is then I know I have raised a healthy animal that will be a worthwhile addition to the milking herd one day.[8]

When a heifer is five to seven months old, she is branded, to identify her as belonging to Shamrock, and then dehorned. The latter is an unpleasant but absolutely necessary task, as an adult cow with horns is hazardous not only to pen mates but also to herself. The younger she is when branded and dehorned, the sooner she is likely to recuperate. Normally it takes only a week or two for a heifer to regain her appetite and return to eating the grain and hay that supply her body with the nutrients she needs. When at nine or ten months of age she weighs 500 pounds, the heifer and her contemporaries in the herd are trucked to a farm in Oakley, Idaho, where for the next several months they are given special feed to make them gain weight. According to Susie Upton, "We grow these heifers out in Idaho because we do not have the space to raise them [and] it is less expensive to feed them there."[9]

SUSIE UPSON

Once [the heifers] reach 850 pounds, at 17 to 18 months, they are at the proper maturity to breed. The heifers are then moved to a pen with registered Holstein bulls to be bred naturally. Once the heifer is diagnosed pregnant by a veterinarian, she is left to eat and browse about at will until she is seven months pregnant [and] is ready to make her long journey back to Arizona and the dairy farm. She is loaded on a truck and makes the 19-hour ride back with her contemporaries. When she reaches the farm, she is put in a pen with other cows who are anywhere from seven to nine months pregnant. Here she awaits the birth of her calf, which will begin another cycle. The heifer now becomes a cow in the milking herd....[10]

Breeding cattle "naturally" was normally the Shamrock way. But experimentation took place to produce what Bob Whitehurst, general manager of Shamrock Farms for fourteen years ending in 1994, called a historic first: the birth "of our first Guernsey calf conceived by 'embryo transplantation.' "[11]

ROBERT J. "BOB" WHITEHURST
Retired General Manager, Shamrock Farms Company

This purebred Guernsey calf was conceived in her biological mother on May 11, 1987, and flushed from her mother and implanted in a Shamrock Holstein heifer who served as the surrogate mother and delivered the calf on February 9, 1988....She has a full sister born February 11, 1988. Genetically speaking, these are the finest Guernsey calfs ever born at Shamrock Farms.[12]

Change and improvement remained components of Shamrock's long-term planned growth, and the Chandler Heights farm underwent gradual but continual change almost from day one. In 1993, for example, an elaborate water-cooled fan system was installed in all the corrals to provide some relief from summer heat. According to Frances, the system was designed "to cut down the death loss, help pregnancy—cows don't conceive when it's really, really hot—and raise milk production."[13]

A year later, according to the *Shamrock News*, further expansion took place:

Shamrock Farms has...completed a new commodity barn to help accommodate some of this growth. The old barn was a simple structure with one side open and no dividing walls. The new commodity barn has both sides accessible and has six dividing walls per side. The cows require quite a variety in their diet to ensure both their health and good production. Besides grains such as corn and barley, the cows might have cottonseed, beet pulp, hominy, malt, pellets, almond hulls and mill run. Depending on their lactation cycle, the feed might also contain cow mineral, molasses, tallow and meat and bone meal. The cows will also receive hay, haylage, which is chopped and fermented hay, or maybe corn silage, which is chopped and fermented corn stalks.

Many of the ingredients can be mixed ahead of time to form premixes which help to speed the feeding process. The commodity barn accommodates storage of the premixes as well as the initial ingredients. Instead of having several piles of different feed far apart, the feed is now centralized but separated by product. The new commodity barn reduces waste by reducing water damage and preventing the feed from being blown all over the desert in a wind storm. Frank Boyce and Larry Ricks, who both designed the new barn, are pleased with the savings in feed costs and the flexibility it affords in feed management.[14]

By the mid-'90s, Shamrock could boast of having the largest dairy farm west of the Mississippi and one of the highest producing daily herd averages in Arizona.

NORMAN McCLELLAND

It is obviously easier to have a higher daily herd average with a smaller number of cows, but I believe that this size dairy farm, 6,000 head of cattle, can produce milk for the least cost per hundredweight. Certainly there is a trend across America for milk production to move from its traditional home in the northern United States to the sunshine states of California, Arizona, New Mexico, and Texas. There are many reasons to explain this trend, the most important being the less intensive capital investment required for corral type feeding and housing of dairy cattle.[15]

As far back as the 1940s, Shamrock was a principal participant in dairy cattle shows where Guernseys were exhibited. Ribbons were won at state fairs in Arizona and New Mexico, at county fairs in Fresno, California, and Tucson and at regional and national cattle shows as far afield as Iowa, Wisconsin, and Washington State. Shamrock was also involved in promoting Guernsey cattle through auctions in Arizona and other western states and in generally promoting the breeding, registration, and testing of Guernsey cattle. In 1979, one of the three years that Norman was its president, the American Guernsey Cattle Club held its annual convention in Arizona. A convention highlight was a visit to Shamrock Farms where club members could see the prizewinning cows of the Shamrock herd and observe how the facilities and cattle were maintained.

That same year, Shamrock received six first-place blue ribbons, six second-place red ribbons, five third-place white ribbons, and the coveted Herdsman Ribbon, won by the Shamrock Farms crew for cleanliness of the animals, stalls, aisles, and equipment. Over the years since then, Shamrock's show herd kept the names of both the dairy division and the Guernsey breed before the public, helping to sustain awareness of the Guernsey cow as a symbol of quality.

Chapter Eight

A Brand-New Business

By the mid-'60s, having successfully followed its mandate of planned growth, Shamrock had captured about 35 percent of the dairy market in Arizona, with total sales approaching $18 million. But business projections began to indicate that future expansion would not be occurring at the same rate as in the past. For a company that had once promulgated the slogan "Something More Than a Bottle of Milk," a company grown accustomed to growth on a grand scale—in a state that had been experiencing an enormous post-World War II boom—the future suddenly presented a limited horizon; that is, of course, if the company were to remain solely in the business it knew best. But what beyond dairying could it do? How could it diversify effectively?

"We hadn't really peaked," Dave Hall insisted, "but looking ahead, we felt that increasing our dairy volume in the state and getting more business would take a long, long time. We had a lot of people, back in the sixties who were young and eager to grow, to keep things moving. We were very concerned about what our next step should be."[1]

Ezra Crandall, a Ph.D. from the elite Wharton School of Business at the University of Pennsylvania, was invited to conduct a seminar for Shamrock's management group—a weekend-long marathon away from the company offices. The purpose was to explore various directions in which Shamrock's future could be plotted. Norman and Frances attended, along with Bill Parker, Tom Stafford, and Dave Hall, among others.

DAVE HALL

I remember the first question Crandall asked when we got to the Mountain Shadows Resort: "What business are you in?" And I thought, "My God, he doesn't even know we're in the dairy business! Oh boy, this is going to be one of *those* meetings." But Crandall was a facilitator, a professional trained to ask questions. In getting answers, he drew a lot of things out of us, got us to talking—and thinking. We talked about what we did and what we could do and what other companies had done. He led us into areas of discussion we wouldn't have ventured into on our own. At the end of the third day, when our meeting ended, Norman and I had become convinced we weren't really just a dairy company; we were a refrigerated delivery company. A whole new world suddenly opened up for us.[2]

The decision to get into food service in an important and aggressive way was a direct result of Shamrock's awareness that the company should not limit itself to doing business as a dairy. As soon as the management team began to think in terms of being in refrigerated delivery, Shamrock's business outlook began to change. Recalled Dave Hall, "We started thinking, well, we don't have to deliver only dairy products; we can deliver other things too."[3]

DAVE HALL

Our first opportunity to get into the food-service business came in 1966 when we decided to purchase Dora Brothers Distributing Company, which was located in Globe, Arizona, and served the north-central portion of the state, including the Show Low Mountains and the big Apache Indian Reservation.[4]

Once a decision had been made for Shamrock to acquire his company, Joe Dora became understandably impatient for the deal to be consummated.

NORMAN McCLELLAND

Joe's attorney was Barry DeRose, who represented the White Mountain Apache Indian tribe. Our attorney, Riney Salmon, also represented the Salt River Project. The Indians and Salt River were squabbling about water rights, and there was no love lost between the two attorneys.

We had set January 1, 1966, as Shamrock's takeover day, but when we could see that we weren't going to get the written agreement by then, Joe and I just shook hands and went ahead with the deal—without a contract. The attorneys were not too happy with either of us, as the actual written agreement wasn't signed for another six weeks, but it all worked out fine for both sides.[5]

At the time of the purchase, Joe Dora's sales volume was about $2 million a year, 10 percent ($200,000) of which was in frozen foods. That $200,000 was 100 percent retail—product delivered to stores to be resold. Joe Dora was a Borden's milk distributor for the Yuma, White Mountain, and Coolidge areas; he was also a member of the Frozen Food Forum of America, an organization of food distributors who shared a number of common labels. One of them was Frosty Acres.

NORMAN McCLELLAND

The Frozen Food Forum had been formed in 1954 by five distributors located in the southeastern part of the U.S. The reason: Following World War II, as the frozen-food business gathered momentum, distributors found themselves developing and selling more and more national brand merchandise to their customers. When the volume of business to a particular customer rose to a level of some importance, the national company would often step in and begin selling directly to the customer, bypassing a distributor.

Drawn together in hopes of preventing this in the future, the distributors decided to establish an organization that would package and sell its own product—under common labels that each member-distributor would own and control exclusively in his territory. The founders conceived of the group as a fraternal organization in which each member could share its successes and help each other grow. Thus each member of the Frozen Food Forum received one share of common stock and one vote.

When Shamrock bought Joe Dora's share of stock, the Forum's board of directors was asked to approve our membership. Fortunately, we were accepted. Had we been a national company competing against other Forum members, or if we had also been a manufacturer marketing under a national label, we would not have been eligible to join as a voting member.[6]

Despite an agreed-upon desire to broaden the scope of its business, Shamrock had purchased Dora Brothers primarily for its dairy-distribution system in Pinal County (Superior, Miami, and Globe) and in northeastern Arizona (Show Low, Springerville, St. John, McNary, and Eager). But as a kind of bonus the company also acquired a toehold in the distribution of frozen-food items, most of which were packaged for sale to grocery stores.

Frozen foods were not a significant part of Dora Brothers' business, thus were not high on Shamrock's list of concerns, but Joe Dora himself had his eye on the future—beyond the current sales figures. He, more than anyone, realized the importance and uniqueness of the Frozen Food Forum and the potential value of that single share of stock Shamrock had received in acquiring his company. He strongly urged Shamrock to be an active constituent in the Forum.

DAVE HALL

Our first thought was that we didn't want to distribute frozen foods, but Joe kept insisting that one of us should attend the next Frozen Food Forum stockholders' meeting. I finally agreed to do it and, I must say, came away very impressed. Everybody I met, food distributors as opposed to dairymen, represented a company that was not only profitable but growing. Those guys were tough, and they had incredible spirit, but the more I talked with them the more I realized that a lot of what we were doing was way, way ahead of them, even though we hadn't been in the food business.

All our trucks were refrigerated by then, whereas they were just getting into refrigerated trucks; we were using IBM for processing—we weren't into computers yet—and they were still doing everything by hand. Even our personnel practices seemed advanced, by comparison, for our employee relations were way ahead of theirs. Our growth had been predicated upon our ability to assign major responsibilities to our people and judiciously follow up. But the men I met didn't know what I was talking about. Still, they were *up* because they were really growing. And I was suddenly saying to myself, "Hey, this might be something."

It was becoming clear that food service in general and frozen foods in particular were potentially very profitable and could be a major outlet for our expanding needs, specifically our need to grow, because it would tap our strength in the refrigerated delivery business. We knew we weren't interested in dealing with retail stores, so we dropped the retail items Joe had been selling and focused instead on delivering frozen foods to food-service establishments: restaurants, hotels, hospitals, drive-ins, school cafeterias. Institutional food service was the area that was growing then.

The benefits of being part of Frosty Acres were significant in our case because we were starting out with no prior knowledge of food service. Because of our new affiliation, we were able to align ourselves with a group that now numbers eighty-four members, each of whom owns a single share of stock, just as we do. Because we were not competing with one another, we were able to talk freely about our concerns—what products to carry, how to make a profit—and take advantage of a centralized buying office that assured us of quality as well as consistency in pricing.[7]

NORMAN MCCLELLAND

This was a completely new business for Shamrock, and we had to learn it from scratch. Since the bulk of Dora Brothers' sales were to retail stores, frozen foods were routinely delivered along with dairy products in the same trucks. Although the full-service concept of dairy delivery was predominant then, we soon made two important decisions that took our business practices in another direction. First, food sales would be divorced from the dairy operation and run as a separate enterprise. Second, we would divide the full-service sales/delivery functions. The selling function would be handled by a sales professional; delivery would be the responsibility of a professional driving a delivery vehicle. This new system proved highly efficient, enabling Shamrock to make a sizable increase in the volume of sales and delivery per person, and also to make year-by-year productivity improvements in the marketing and delivery areas of our business.[8]

DAVE HALL

I think that during the first couple of years we were in the Forum I visited almost every Frosty Acres distributor there was—from New Mexico to New Jersey. It was the first really big wholesale or food-service buying co-op in the country. We stayed mostly in frozen foods from 1966 until 1970, and by that time Frosty Acres had gone into canned goods. So we followed suit.[9]

Harold Hornbeck recalled the events that followed the acquisition of Dora Brothers. He had been hired by Shamrock as a sales merchandiser in 1964, acting as liaison between the dairy and its supermarket clients to make sure that enough milk was ordered and then rotated properly in the dairy case. But within two years his job was to change.

HAROLD HORNBECK
Former sales merchandiser of dairy products

On January 1, 1966, Norman McClelland and I left Tucson to do an inventory of the Coolidge vault of frozen foods and dairy products. When we took over distribution of frozen-food products in that area, Norman advised me, "Run this business as you would a grocery store—make money." When we first got into the business, we were handling approximately fifteen items but had no confirmed price list; thus we had no idea what to sell things for. A short time later, Shamrock Dairy purchased Portion Pak Foods in the Tucson area, and this put us into the frozen-food business in the southern part of the state.[10]

Once Shamrock had become established in food service, Norman asked Dave to take charge of it. Dave had some reservations, because that division was so small and he still had responsibilities in the dairy, but he agreed to it. He hadn't grown up in the dairy business as Norman had but, he noted, "I sure learned a lot in the first fifteen years I was with the company."[11] After a few more years he was thoroughly absorbed in the food division, particularly when it, too, began to grow.

DAVE HALL

With Norman's encouragement, I became very active in acquisitions. I handled almost all of them from the late sixties on. Norman liked my being the point person in such matters, as I had the ability to make people feel that we would treat them honestly and with integrity, that we wouldn't cheat them—and would be up front with them—and that if they wanted to become part of our company we would welcome them. I had a knack for doing that. Somebody had to open the doors on these things, and I enjoyed that role. Norman would come in with the final say.[12]

A few months after the Dora Brothers acquisition and Norman's decision to separate the dairy and food-service divisions, Shamrock Institutional Foods was launched. The new entity began life in leased space in a public warehouse in Phoenix, but in April 1966, twenty acres of industrial development land was purchased on West Encanto, near the dairy, to use for future expansion, which would begin taking place within a few years. Eventually this became the home of Shamrock Institutional Foods and its futuristic mega-warehouse.

DAVE HALL

In the summer of 1969 we were able to acquire Quality Foods in Tucson, a small company that distributed mainly canned goods. We kept the company's small warehouse and operated out of it for a year so we could learn a bit about canned goods. But the volume was so inconsequential we didn't learn very much.

However, in 1970 we had the opportunity to purchase Arizona Frozen Foods, which was probably the largest food-service distributor in Arizona at the time. While their name certainly confirmed their particular commitment, they had also maintained a meat operation and had been distributing canned goods, paper goods, and disposables for over a year, which we saw as another opportunity to expand our business. We closed the small warehouses in Tucson and Flagstaff and moved everything to Phoenix, operating out of Arizona Frozen Foods' leased facilities, which were in the old Crystal Ice Plant on West McDowell.

One good thing to emerge from this acquisition, aside from gaining additional opportunities to expand our business, was being able to bring Donald Van Wormer to Shamrock. He had been Arizona Frozen Foods' vice president in charge of purchasing.[13]

DONALD "DON" VAN WORMER
Retired Vice President and General Manager of Arizona Foods Division

I had heard a lot of good things about Shamrock, so I was looking forward to their coming in. I had some friends at the company, was well acquainted with the way it operated, and knew how highly respected Shamrock was in the community. I also knew it to be growth-oriented, which at my age then was what I was looking for. As far as I was concerned, it was going to be a good marriage, because I felt I really did have something to offer them.

The president of Arizona Frozen Foods, who happened to be my cousin, had reached an age where he didn't feel he wanted to go any further in the business. We either had to sell out or get out. We had maybe two or three hundred items at most; we also had our own manufacturing meat plant where we processed steaks and hamburgers. I was in charge of that when I first started in the business. Shamrock also acquired that part of the operation, but what they bought primarily when they acquired my company was goodwill. We didn't own anything. All of our facilities were leased.[14]

Don worked in purchasing for Shamrock until 1977, when he was named general manager of the foods division. At the time his company had been acquired, its total annual volume was around $5 million. By the time he retired, in 1988, it was $167 million. Six years later, the volume had skyrocketed to $300 million.

Another well-choreographed and equally significant acquisition was that of Meadow Gold Dairy in Glendale, Arizona, confirming the fact that Shamrock's managed growth would continue to be shared by both of its divisions. Meadow Gold's intricate early history was recalled by Edith Stallings, an employee of Meadow Gold, then of Shamrock, for a total of twenty-five years.

EDITH STALLINGS
Former employee of Meadow Gold and Shamrock Dairy

This plant was founded in 1916 as the Pacific Creamery Company. For a few years it manufactured and distributed canned milk under the trade name Armour, then in the early 1920s was shut down. It remained out of production until 1930, when it was purchased by Dudley Webster, former owner of the Borden's plant in Tempe and the Maricopa Creamery in Phoenix. Renamed Webster's Dairy and remodeled extensively during a two-year period, the plant began producing longhorn cheese, butter, and buttermilk in 1933.

In 1936, Webster's began processing and bottling milk in glass bottles and, later, may well have become first in the nation to package fresh milk in paper cartons. Twenty years later the dairy plant was purchased by Beatrice Foods Company and reestablished as Webster's Meadow Gold and Associated Dairy Products.[15]

Another of the Meadow Gold employees to be absorbed by Shamrock was Jim Sheffer, who recounted why his former company had been sold. After Beatrice Foods Company operated it as a subsidiary for more than a dozen years, the Federal Trade Commission ruled that Beatrice was monopolizing certain businesses throughout the country and would have to divest itself of no fewer than five of its companies, including all of its Arizona holdings.

Meadow Gold was sold to Sea Containers, Inc., a London-based firm whose main function was to ship frozen foods overseas in huge containers. These were self-containers that froze their contents automatically and kept everything at freezing temperatures. Thus food could be container-stored from the place of production to each destination point without use of the usual refrigeration methods. The dairy became known as the Coldwrap Foods Division, even though it continued to market products under the Meadow Gold label.

Jim Sheffer reported that with food-industry people in charge, rather than experienced dairymen, a number of changes took place that made life difficult for former Webster's employees. But within months the acquisition proved an unhappy alliance for Coldwrap too; its management decided that they were insufficiently informed about the dairy industry and should get out of it. According to Jim, some insiders at the time opined that a sizable amount of dairy profit was being siphoned off to pump up other areas of the company. Whatever the circumstances, the company was ripe for sale when Shamrock tendered an offer.

Out of this 1971 transaction came a number of key accounts, including Associated Grocers. Many employees remained after the acquisition, some of the equipment was transferred to Shamrock, but the plant itself was shuttered permanently.[16]

Ted Springer, a small-business consultant when he was hired full time by Shamrock in 1962, remembered how he absorbed the impact of the Meadow Gold purchase.

THEODORE M. "TED" SPRINGER
Retired dairy plant accountant

When Norman announced that we were acquiring Meadow Gold, one of the major dairies in the state, it was almost unbelievable—the amount of volume that would be added to our company. Here again, he called upon the Shamrock family, and it certainly rose to the occasion. Meadow Gold was absorbed so smoothly that I don't know of any customer who ever missed Meadow Gold product. One of the most important things I learned at Shamrock was that change would be a way of life. Anyone unable to endure changing conditions would not perform successfully here.

One of Norman's philosophies that contribute greatly to our advantage in the marketplace is that we strive to serve the customer at a fair price for a fair profit. And this philosophy of not gouging the customer, I think, was one of the major reasons for our phenomenal success in the food business. The growth we experienced resulted in part from foresightedness and all the other attributes that go with good management, but I think it also resulted from a basic concept that has been a major factor throughout Shamrock's history—that of everyone's working together, pulling together to do the job right.[17]

Frances McClelland summed up the impact of Meadow Gold in just eight words: "It was the smoothest acquisition we ever made."[18]

Shamrock's ability to absorb a company with ease, to transplant its well-honed culture and management style, would soon be thoroughly tested with two major food service acquisitions. Together they would constitute their own separate divison, one that would open up a new geographical area for Shamrock sales and distribution, be recognized as a landmark along the road of planned growth, and become a crucible to test the skills of Shamrock's management team.

Colorado was calling.

*Shamrock Dairy products in the then-new waxed paper cartons
and traditional cream-top bottle, 1947.*

A mechanized glass bottle filler, 1950.

Cottage cheese mixed by hand with a wooden paddle in the Phoenix plant, 1956.

Frances and Norman with their parents in the backyard of the McClelland house on East Lee Street, Tucson, 1948.

The Tucson offices and plant in 1961.

Shamrock Dairy's 40th anniversary celebration open house in Phoenix, 1962.

*His eye on history, John Harty views the steel framework
of the Phoenix plant, 1955.*

*Gathered around Daisy Dawn, a Guernsey champion, during 40th anniversary festivities in
Phoenix, from left to right: Frances Parker, Mrs. Mac's sister; Mrs. Mac; Mr. Mac;
Norman and Frances McClelland; and Bill Parker, 1962.*

Norman and Cliff Knight look on as Hap Muller holds Shamrock Neslekcim Fortune's Fancy, named All American Cow at the World Dairy Expo in Madison, Wisconsin, 1972.

Shamrock Foods Company's Board of Directors, 1984, left to right: Oliver Stallings, assistant secretary; William J. Parker, chairman; Norman McClelland, president; Frances McClelland, secretary-treaasurer; David Hall, senior vice president.

Chapter Nine

Colorado—From the Beginning

*D*ave Hall, who had been reticent at first about the Frosty Acres affiliation and about Shamrock's involvement in food service, became, in time, a Frosty Acres and food-service enthusiast.

DAVE HALL

The buying power of eighty-four members combined was obviously much greater than that of any one member individually, but the biggest benefit we probably received from Frosty Acres was being in an association along with other companies whose situations were similar to our own.

Particularly during our first years in food service, we visited a great many companies throughout the United States, learning what they did right, observing what they did wrong, and applying that knowledge to our own business. Many of the thoughts and practices that have proved successful for Shamrock Foods were a direct result of these visits and of what we learned from other Frosty Acres members.[1]

Meeting and talking with other Frosty Acres stockholders on an informal basis have solidified some friendships and, not surprisingly, set the stage for some business alliances important to Shamrock. It was through Frosty Acres that Dave remembered becoming acquainted with John Kennedy, president of Denver-based Inland Frosted Foods.

John and two partners had organized and incorporated the company in 1945. Their assets then consisted solely of the $10,000 the three partners had been able to pool plus $15,000 from a handful of stockholders and one vehicle to service the customers. At the time it seemed a risky enterprise: World War II was just ending and the future was uncertain. The frozen-food industry in Colorado was so minuscule that not even a supermarket chain as important as Safeway offered frozen products. To dim the prospects even further, the usually prescient *Wall Street Journal* was predicting that frozen foods would never be popular.

What no financial or sociological soothsayer could have predicted was the release of consumer demand for convenience that had been sidelined by the war. This, coupled with a rising birthrate, later recognized as a baby boom, changed the prospects for Inland Frosted Foods and for countless other firms across the land. Within twenty-five years, with John Kennedy as president and general manager, Inland would have more than a dozen trucks, including two large semis, would serve the entire eastern slope of Colorado and south-eastern Wyoming as a frozen-food distributor, establish a Colorado Springs branch, and employ about fifty people. By this time, John was in search of growth of another order.

DAVE HALL

At Frosty Acres stockholder meetings, John and I always seemed to sit together—because he was from the West and I was from the West—so we got to know each other pretty well. I came to think highly of him. One day, in a casual conversation, John confided that he would be happy to sell Inland Frosted Foods if he could find a company he felt confident would take care of his employees. Like

Norman's dad, he ran the company paternalistically, wanting to do things for his employees but lacking the means to do so. He couldn't offer them health insurance, profit sharing, or retirement pay, which he knew Shamrock provided.

"If you're ever interested in moving up into Denver, you're the kind of company I'd like to become part of," he said. I immediately arranged a visit, reviewed John's financial statements, and recommended to Norman that we negotiate to buy the company. It was one of the few times in our history when there was available cash to invest. We had no purpose or overall plan at the time—beyond wanting to grow and expand and feeling this would be an excellent opportunity for Shamrock.

John didn't own any land, buildings, or equipment. He rented everything; even his trucks were leased. But though his was a fairly small company doing $1.5 million in sales, he had a lot of good employees. Their loyalty matched John's paternalism. He was very much the father.[2]

Bill Parker helped make it possible for us to acquire Inland Frosted Foods. At board of directors meetings he was always supportive of our plans and schemes. When Norman and I proposed a possible acquisition, Bill was invariably the first one at the table to say, "I think we ought to do it." The Colorado deal was the biggest one to date that we had ever presented to the board, for the asking price represented a lot of money for our company then. But Bill Parker was the first one to say, "I think we ought to do it."[3]

In July 1970, Shamrock Foods Company formally acquired Inland Frosted Foods, opening up a frontier in a new area, the Rocky Mountain region, and adding to Shamrock's most recent category of growth, food service. "I look back now," said Dave years later, "and I think how naive we were, because going to another state didn't bother me in the least. It didn't bother Norman or Bill

Parker either. Actually, we didn't really acquire anything there except the sales organization, because everything was leased."[4]

Within five years Shamrock would extend Inland Frosted Foods' volume to $5 million and expand the company itself, reinforcing its Colorado base. In 1973 the National Commission Company was acquired from Harvey Klunder. A small company, it sold groceries primarily, and canned goods, too, from a warehouse in Colorado Springs that Shamrock remodeled extensively and continued to operate until 1976, when all Colorado operations were centralized in Denver. Merging the two companies provided statewide coverage not only for merchandising frozen foods but groceries and related items as well. "Harvey Klunder was a fine guy," said Dave. "He stayed on, working under John Kennedy to manage the new firm, which became known as Inland National Foods in the Colorado Springs area."[5]

Solidifying Inland's foothold in northern Colorado and eastern Wyoming was the acquisition of Stehman Distributing Company of Greeley, Colorado. That was in 1976, the year Sid Schwartz Distributing Company was also acquired. It carried meat products, a small line of groceries, plus some produce.

By far Shamrock's biggest acquisition in Colorado, the one that would secure its future growth in the region, was that of United Food Service, which was merged with Inland to form Inland-United Food Service in 1975 with John Kennedy as its president and United's Alfred L. "Fritz" Covillo as senior vice president. "John remained with the expanded company for only a short time," Dave recalled. "Health problems compelled him to retire. So in 1976 I moved up to Denver as president of the company and stayed there about two years. Then more and more management duties were turned over to Fritz."[6]

Fritz's father, James Covillo, had started the family company in 1915, becoming the first wholesale produce distributor in Denver. He used a horse-drawn wagon to display his products and transport them to his customers from the open-air City Market (located between West Eleventh Avenue and Speer, from Champa to Stout streets) and the Farmer's Market (which ran along the Cherry Creek River from Champa to California streets). For James Covillo, it was a proud day when a new gasoline-powered truck could be purchased to facilitate further growth. James had been one of the first Colorado distributors to purchase a truck for use in the produce business.

After World War II James turned the produce operation over to his three sons: Ernest, Vincent, and Fritz. It was hardly a major enterprise at the time; the entire business fit neatly into a twenty-by-forty-foot stall in the Denargo Market, a wholesale-produce yard built in Denver by the Union Pacific Railroad Company. This stall provided warehouse and office space, and housed a ten-by-twelve-foot refrigerator, a rest room, and a small rectangle into which the company truck could be squeezed for indoor parking. Covillo products were still being sold right off this truck at the time.

By 1970, Covillo Brothers Produce, as it was called then, occupied between seven and ten stalls in the Denargo Market and had expanded to become a seventeen-truck operation. In growing their company, the brothers had acquired several small wholesale peddling routes, including the Piscatella Produce, Biggerstaff Food, and Zarlengo Food companies. But what really marked a step up in potential business was the deal Covillo Brothers made with Grand Junction Fruit in 1970, a merger that provided an immediate increase in product lines and inventories and necessitated designing and remodeling a space to create new quarters. The newly formed company was named United Food Service.

It was a merger of two companies that had experienced similar histories, for the founder of Grand Junction Fruit Co., Max Mozer, had begun shipping fresh fruit to Denver from Grand Junction, Colorado, in the earliest days of wholesale produce distribution. At one point he had operated a fruit stand on Fifteenth Street, between Welton and Fremont, in Denver and later opened a business on Seventh Avenue, between Kalamath and Sante Fe. With sons Sidney and Louis as partners, Max had also expanded his business over the years. At the time of the merger with Covillo Brothers Produce, his company was handling produce, frozen foods, and a very limited supply of dry-food products.

United Food Service, a partnership involving two families (three brothers plus a father and two sons), began doing business on July 1, 1970. Before taking over their new facility on Denver's East Fortieth Avenue, the six partners had collaborated on a design for the space, to make it totally modern and fully able to accommodate their plans for future expansion. To assume an even stronger position in the competitive food-service industry, United then acquired Al's Produce (from Al Naracci), Politano Food Company (from Tony Politano Sr., and Jr.), Stamison Foods (from Richard Gacatta), and C. T. Fluken Produce (from C. T. and John Fluken).

On paper, the Covillo-Grand Junction partnership made a great deal of sense, but the everyday fact of it was that the two families often clashed on how the new company should be operated.

DAVE HALL

I was very impressed with the operation, its cleanliness, the lack of spoilage, and, in particular, its $10 million volume. But the management climate was intolerable; the partners barely spoke to one another. They had only agreed on two things, as far as I could tell— first, to merge, and second, to sell. Otherwise they fought like animals. I met with the Covillos on one side of the office; then I'd go to the other side to talk with the Mozers. They were all good people; they just didn't get along. The two Mozer boys didn't get along with each other, and their father was always mad at both of them.

I knew we would not retain all six partners—if the deal went through, it would be nothing but *me* being a peacemaker. But when the Mozer brothers asked point-blank whom we would hire, I told them honestly that we would probably hire just two—and only because of their knowledge of the produce business, which we had not been in before.

Ultimately, after making the deal, we did offer to hire two of the partners: Fritz Covillo, who functioned very successfully in sales, and his brother Ernie, who really knew the produce business. For health reasons, unfortunately, Ernie had to decline the opportunity. One important, though secondary, reason Shamrock was eager to acquire this company was that United Food Service owned land, buildings and trucks, and until that time we had not actually owned anything in Denver. This single acquisition provided us with a very substantial Colorado base plus a fleet of trucks. It was one of the few times, I think, that our management group had really planned things.[7]

United Food Service Company was an amalgam of different and disparate companies. It flouished, but it was functioning like a multiheaded monster when it was acquired by Inland. "We had a lot of problems in Colorado,"[8] Frances McClelland pointed out, alluding to what was essentially a clash between the Shamrock culture ("looking out for people, taking care of them,"[9] said Norman) and the Fritz Covillo philosophy ("the company first, then the employees,"[10] according to Frances). Fritz had a demanding ego and a flamboyant style; he also had, till then, an astonishing success record that helped make his company an attractive purchase. But after the acquisition he continued to operate as he once had, creating tension between himself and Shamrock and confusion among the members of his own staff.

One of the first persons to take up the challenge of Colorado, after Dave Hall, was Charles Andrews, who had been hired in 1964 as Shamrock Dairy's wholesale sales manager after a twenty-two-year career with Meadow Gold. "Shamrock had been damn tough competitors," said Chuck, "but I knew them to be a fine company, a believable company. They tell you they're going to do something, they do it. They were never a bunch of price-cutters. The way they built and held their business was through *relationships* with their customers. I checked this company out very thoroughly with grocery people I was acquainted with, with some city people who were familiar with the operation, and with some employees as well. And I never ran into anyone who had anything but praise for them."[11]

The only naysayer, predictably, was Chuck's own boss at Meadow Gold, who insisted Shamrock's success was a fluke that would last only another year or two, at which point the company could be bought for ten cents on the dollar. "I knew better," said Chuck. "I was out in the marketplace and was always getting hit with some of Shamrock's merchandising techniques. They did a great job." [12] Even so, Chuck was reluctant at first to make the change.

CHARLES "CHUCK" ANDREWS
Retired Vice President of Shamrock Foods Company

I'd seen what some of the big national companies would do: hire a man just to get him off the market. I wanted to make sure that didn't happen to me. I had a family to feed; I didn't want somebody to just move me off the market. So I said to Norman, "Mr. McClelland, I need you to give me a contract, a ten-year written contract." He said he'd never given anyone a contract, and insisted that his word was as good as anyone's signature. I believed him but continued to press him for an agreement in writing. I still felt a need to protect myself.

I think that's the only time I ever really irritated Norman with what I requested, but he said OK. He gave me a signed contract, and I carried it around in my briefcase for four or five months. By then I knew I'd made the right move. I could tell that all the people I dealt with had accepted me, even though I had been a competitor. And Norman always stood right in back of me supporting whatever action I felt we had to take. I could see that I really was needed, with or without a contract, so one day I walked into his office and said, "Here, we don't need this," and so we tore it up right then. [13]

When Bill Parker announced his wish to retire in Tucson, Norman knew whom to turn to. Chuck Andrews was asked to move to Tucson to run that operation as general manager. His right-hand man, Derrell Fairfield, took over in Tucson when Chuck returned to Phoenix to become general manager of the foods division after Shamrock purchased Arizona Frozen Foods in 1970. Don Van Wormer was in purchasing, feeling uncertain about his role in the newly merged operation as well as where his career was taking him. But Don's patience and loyalty to his new boss would ultimately pay off.

CHUCK ANDREWS

On New Year's Day 1977 I got a phone call from Dave Hall. It was about seven o'clock in the morning. "Chuck," he said, "come down and have a cup of coffee with me at the restaurant." He meant the one on Central Avenue near where I lived. I agreed to meet him, and the minute I walked in, I knew there was trouble. "Chuck," he said, "Norman and I want you to go to Colorado. We've got some problems up there. Our losses are high, and we've got to get them under control. That's why I need to have you there." I dreaded telling my wife, Hazel. She and I loved the home we had, and even planned to make it our retirement home, but I knew she would understand that if the company needed to have me move to Denver, we'd have to do it.

Dave understood my concern about making this move, but insisted he really did need me in Colorado. "Whom do you have here in Phoenix?" he wanted to know. I didn't have to think twice. There was only one choice: Don Van Wormer.[14]

Later in January , when Chuck moved to Denver, Don became general manager of the Arizona Foods Division. He remained in this position until his retirement in 1988. For Chuck, what started out as a four-year stint in Colorado ultimately stretched to five, as he strived to turn Inland-United into a Shamrock company. Fritz Covillo had been on vacation in Hawaii when Chuck arrived in

Denver. When he returned, said Chuck, "I met him, sat down and talked with him. I told him, 'I want you to join me in running this company.' Fritz had hoped to be made general manager himself, but it was no surprise to him that if Norman and Dave had sent me to Denver, they had moved me up there as general manager."[15]

CHUCK ANDREWS

I told Fritz the first thing I wanted to do was have a meeting with all of his people, all of his warehouse people and all of his drivers. We got together at seven o'clock one evening, and I told them, "I was sent up here to work with you people." I didn't say as general manager or anything else because it didn't make any difference. The important thing was to hash it out, to let the guys know that their organization was not returning a profit, and that *I* was there to see that it did. It took about seven months to get things straightened out and to get a little ahead. I went down to a quarterly financial meeting and presented a ten-dollar bill to Norman. That's all there was, but it showed that we finally had turned a profit.[16]

Chuck's problems were far from over. Two disgruntled employees were continually challenging his management and within two years had joined forces with representatives of the Teamsters' organization in an attempt to unionize the company. A lot of pressure was brought to bear, a vote was taken, and a majority of the employees decided in favor of the union. "But in the negotiations," Chuck pointed out, "our company offered them more money than what competing companies were paying people who were already in the union. The union wanted us to actually lower our offer—because it put them in a bad position. If they had gone along with what we offered, they would have had an uproar on their hands from union people in other companies. We played it smart, though, and it killed them deader than a mackerel."[17]

That didn't happen quickly, and it didn't happen without pain. A strike was called. "We told the union we would not give them a closed shop and we refused to take payroll deductions for their monthly fee," said Chuck. "The people who voted not to unionize were going to be working right here; we were not going to force anyone to join a union."[18]

CHUCK ANDREWS

They struck on a Saturday, so Fritz and I got on the telephone Sunday night. We had about fifty employees, including the pickers and all. We told them we expected them to be on the job the next day and said, "If you don't show up, we'll have to replace you." Then a storm hit, a blinding snowstorm. I came to the plant about three-thirty that morning, and Fritz and I made coffee. We took hot coffee to the guys on the line, and I told them, "Look, you guys are not dressed for this kind of weather. You're all going to be sick. Why don't you come on into the plant?"

We did that every day. We treated them nice; we didn't blast any one of them. With the snowstorm hitting them in the face like that, day after day, we could see them starting to weaken. At the same time a lot of profanity was flying around, and within a few days some threats of violence were reported. We called the police and, boy, they were there in a minute and a half. "Look," they said. "We will not put up with any violence. We'll put all of you in jail if we have to." So they stopped and they dropped it, and that seemed to just take the life out of them.

Meanwhile, everyone else was pitching in, even Norman. He was there, too, cutting lettuce, riding the tugger, lifting those cases. He was right in there with them. But the strike really hurt us. Business fell off drastically because we had really poor service there for a while. Finally, after the fourteenth day, the strike ended. The men kicked over the fire bucket, one of those old oil drums that was burning scrap to keep them warm, and walked away. They just left. That was it.[19]

When it was clear to Shamrock's management that the Colorado operation could run smoothly and that a new plant would ultimately be needed to handle projected future growth, Chuck was put in charge of selecting the building site and overseeing the new construction. Fritz Covillo took over as general manager of Inland-United, working under Dave Hall as president. Michael Mueller remembered these as troubled times. He had joined the company in sales in 1979, rising first to be Denver district manager and then general sales manager.

MICHAEL "MIKE" MUELLER
Marketing specialist, Colorado Foods Division

I was pretty much a figurehead. I don't think Fritz Covillo wanted anybody but himself to run the sales department. He himself was a consummate salesman, one of the best salespeople you'd ever want to meet. It was very difficult for him to hand over any responsibilities. Everyone who came in contact with him, socially or professionally, liked him. He was that kind of a guy, and he could sell anything to anyone, anytime. All he had to do was turn it on.

I think that if Fritz could have been content being sales manager, he would have been happier, he would have been where he needed to be. But I don't think his ego would have allowed him to do that. He had to be the top banana. However, as general manager he didn't pay much, if any, attention to the other departments. His whole focus was sales, sales, sales. If you had a problem in the warehouse or with trucks, or if you had a problem in Accounting, he didn't want to be involved with it that much. His attitude was, "Just go fix it and leave me alone." He didn't have a great understanding of accounting principles or accounting practices, but his sales staff had a different view; they would have killed for him.

Fritz was kind, generous, and charismatic, but at the same time he also worried a great deal, and the people he worried about most were his salespeople. He was sure that if they weren't in the office at seven o'clock in the morning they'd still be in bed at nine. So every weekday, Monday through Friday, we'd have a 7 A.M. sales meeting.

Fritz had phenomenal power over people. To please him you'd run till you fell down. He brought you in so close that whatever he said was absolute—the law. And one of the things he would say was that there was a constant battle going on between Colorado and Arizona, the two foods divisions.

Honest to God, he would say things like the Colorado division was so much better than the Arizona division. Then he'd talk about all the people down there and how dumb they were. I remember the first time either Norman or David decided that we were going to get together and do some brainstorming. It was just a bunch of district sales managers talking about how to raise gross margins and sell more groceries, but I remember the shock of listening to Bob Wyman and Mike Krueger—both of whom were district sales managers in Phoenix then—and realizing that these people knew a great deal about the food business. Krueger is as brilliant a man as you'll ever run into, and Bob Wyman, salt of the earth, had probably forgotten more than most people know and understand about the food business after twenty-five or thirty years. Which was diametrically opposed to what Fritz had been saying.[20]

The strain of commuting was taking its toll on Dave, as the Colorado operation expanded into sophisticated new quarters in 1983. "We needed to change the position of general manager," said Dave. "We had promoted Fritz out of necessity, but he wasn't able to pull everything together—a new warehouse, a new data-processing system—and I was supervising both Arizona and Colorado. I was flying to Denver on Sunday nights and coming back to Phoenix, exhausted, on Fridays. Having just remarried, I told Norman I thought I'd better quit going up there. 'No,' said Norman, 'you're going to take over as general manager.' So I did, and Jeanne and I moved up there. My task was to turn things around so, once again, we could start making a profit."[21]

Mike Mueller remembers the dismal performance of the Colorado operation during the first months after its move to new facilities. How dismal was made clear at one of the regular financial meetings.

MIKE MUELLER

What happened was that we ended up with an $800,000 loss, after having worked our buns off trying to raise gross profit and get some sales back. I remember sitting in that auditorium feeling absolutely devastated. How could anybody lose $800,000? And I remember Dave getting up and trying to explain how we could look like we looked on the daily financial status report versus what happened when you reviewed the monthly P and L. He tried to explain the whole business about inventory and balances and cash, and one thing and another, and when the meeting was nearly over, Fritz piped up and said, "I don't believe we lost that much money. I can feel when we make money and I believe that it felt last month like we made money."

Fritz was convinced that if you devoted all your time and attention to sales, they would take care of everything—that if you sold enough groceries, all the problems would just go away. Unfortunately, when we moved into the new building, we couldn't sell enough groceries quickly enough, and that was Fritz's undoing, I believe. It was shortly after that meeting when Dave took over the division.

He was welcomed here as a stabilizing force. He may not have known all the answers, but he was an absolute rock on the fact that he was going to get something done. And little bit by little bit and slowly but surely, things began to get better. Dave's presence settled everybody down, so we could begin doing business the Shamrock way. His management style was exactly what this division needed—it was pretty much like his being a marine commander leading troops out of the desert and building an effective team.

With Fritz no longer acting as general manager, or as general sales manager, Dave said to me, "Now you will be expected to manage the sales department. Go do it." So for the first time I had the responsibility and the authority to do my job, but Dave was always a great help. Anytime you had a question, you could count on him for a response. Or if you had a problem, you could talk it out with him.[22]

For Dave Hall, the challenge was to get everyone at last to pull together and to replace those who were not willing or able to do so, making changes as quickly as possible.

DAVE HALL

Basically I am a systems person. I believe you define a job and delegate, then you follow up on it to make sure it's being done. But you let people get the job done their own way. In effect, you build a fence around the job—like, here are the ethics, here are the morals of the company, here is the law of the land, and there is your budget. If you can understand all of that clearly, you can do the job.

We did have to replace a lot of the people in Colorado, but a lot of the changes involved shifting people from one position to another, where they fit a niche better. That helped a lot. By getting everybody to work and pull together, we were also giving our customers more of what they needed. We had a lot to do in that area. Our service levels had dipped; it took us a while to restore customer confidence.

When we moved into the new facility, we put in place a new system of operating the warehouse, and our brand-new data-processing system had a lot of bugs in it. We probably should have taken on one or the other at a time. Anytime you change the habits of people, a period of learning and uncertainty follows, and we had to adjust to not only a new warehouse but also a new operating system. And that was a little too much. We could have done it one at a time—moving into the warehouse but operating as we had been before, then introducing the new system after we had been in there awhile. It would have stretched out the period of adjustment, but we might not have caused our customers so many problems. That's important, you know. It might have cost a little more money, but you don't want to compromise your customer base because that's really all you have.[23]

Norman's son, Kent, began his executive career at Shamrock working under Dave Hall in the Colorado operation, ultimately succeeding him as division president.

MIKE MUELLER

When Kent came to work here, nobody understood anything about data processing or computer technology. You could have walked up and beaned any of us with a modem and we wouldn't have known what it was. When he came aboard we were in the process of developing this new system, and as bright or as dumb as we were as a sales management team—me as the general sales manager plus a whole bunch of district sales managers—we were sure things probably would be just fine for the next ten years or so if we could just get our mission to work. That was as visionary as we were. So if it wasn't for Kent coming along, we would have been dead meat because we would have been so far behind technologically. There would have been no way for us to catch up.

It wasn't yet possible for us as a group to think about what we were going to need more of to sell groceries in five years. We couldn't do it. Kent came along and stopped us all in our tracks. He said, "Hell's coming to breakfast here if we don't do something different," and he began to suggest some options and raise some questions: "What are you going to need to manage the sales in such-and-such account? What are you going to need to manage the sales in your districts?" All of a sudden we began to come up with things — ideas, projections, solutions. That kind of thinking has been real important.

With Fritz, all that was necessary was getting a good sales force and that automatically meant you were a good manager. One of the differences between David and Fritz was that Dave believed budget reform should be a primary objective. With Dave, as with Norman and Kent, there was always the real need to perform well financially. I mean, if you're not making any money, the sardine can gets empty real quick. With Kent on board—and as a manager he was quite different from Dave—the company changed. I think we've come a long way and become a lot better at what we do.[24]

Chapter Ten

Third-Generation Leadership

From Norman McClelland's standpoint, it was never a foregone conclusion that son Kent would become a partner in the family business. In fact, for many years there were strong doubts that he would—fed by Kent's own ambivalance and also by Norman's uncertainty that a career with Shamrock would be appropriate either for his son or for the company. "These family things, sometimes they go on from one generation to the next, and sometimes they don't," Norman observed. "A lot depends on what each person's ambitions are, what he or she hopes for."[1]

As a teenager, Kent worked summers on one or another of the Shamrock farms. "My earliest memories of working are of the farms, and they are my fondest memories," said Kent. "Bill Boyce took me under his wing and taught me how to clean out corrals, drive a tractor, do anything and everything to do with running a farm. I had a blast; I loved it."[2]

Later, as a high school student growing up in Phoenix, and then when he was home from college, Kent spent summers working in the dairy. He was, variously, a garage employee, warehouse order selector, and accounting trainee, and at one point he even manned his own home-delivery route. But taking summer jobs can rarely be equated with making a career decision; during his college years there was still no certainty that he would one day join the family business. After graduating from Colorado College in 1976, however, Kent did become a full-time management trainee in the Phoenix operation, working on the order desk and in route settlement, then in the purchasing and credit departments. Later, during his first stint in Denver, he also acted as office manager.

NORMAN MCCLELLAND

Kent was not a terribly effective office manager; he didn't know what he was doing, and he knew it. We talked about that sometimes. Then he went to graduate school and earned an M.B.A. After getting his degree he went to work for the Mercantile Bank of Canada, and that was really a good experience for him. He made sales calls; he pressed to get real estate loans for the bank; he learned a lot.

At Shamrock, we were content to just go along and see what what would happen. I don't think we talked about it very much, but I do think Kent knew that if he didn't come back at some point soon, we would eventually have to do something with the company. We gave him time to make up his mind because we knew he had to be certain—this would be a lifetime commitment, after all. I didn't know at the time if this was what he wanted to do. He never said he wouldn't join the company or that he would. I felt he needed a chance to explore, to check out other options. I don't think it would have been fair to keep saying, "Well, Kent, you've got to get back here next January, you know, because we need you to do this or that."

Finally, when his job with Mercantile Bank ended, he said he'd like to come back. Colorado was where he was needed then, and I think he liked the idea that Dave Hall was running that division and living in Denver. At any rate, he moved up there and went to work. He started in purchasing, which is the most challenging side of the business. To be successful, you've got to have the right merchandise and you have to be able to promote it properly.[3]

Kent moved to Denver at a time when the Colorado food operation was undergoing its greatest upheaval, the torment of shifting from being a Fritz Covillo organization to a Shamrock organization. And, said Norman, "it was clear that Fritz's way of running an organization and our way was just the difference between night and day. In addition, the Colorado division being 860 miles away from our company headquarters, there was a geographical as well as a cultural divide."[4]

NORMAN MCCLELLAND

Over time it was Kent who pulled that organization together culturally with total quality management plus the other ideas he brought to the company. We encouraged him to attend training seminars and other meetings all over the country, and to bring back inspiration. And from attending those meetings came his impetus for rebuilding the management group in Denver, creating a different way of running the company and a different climate from what had existed before. The change did not take place quickly. Kent lived and worked in Denver for eight years before finally returning to Phoenix.[5]

Like Norman and Frances before him, Kent McClelland was raised with a clear sense that he had been born into a family with deep roots in the dairy business. His earliest memory of his grandfather was, as a three- or four-year-old, sitting on Mr. Mac's lap while the older man ate his breakfast cereal. "He had his own way of showing affection," Kent observed. "'Come to me, boy,' he would say as he took me up in his arms and put me on his knee. 'Can you milk a big coo?' That was a question he would ask me often, in his Irish brogue, when I was a child. The answer, of course, was that I wasn't able to milk a big cow until I was many years older."[6]

WILLIAM KENT MCCLELLAND
President of Shamrock Foods Company

After church on Sunday he and I would sometimes go down
to the dairy, because the cows were there, right on the Tucson property. That's where the herd was; it's also where the milk was
processed and bottled then. It was a treat to be able to go with my
grandfather to see the cows, the calves in the various stages of their
development, and the cows in the milking barn, the maternity barn
and the sick barn. It was fun visiting the farm, and when my grandfather lost his leg and began to use a golf cart, it was fun being
allowed to drive the cart—exciting for me but unnerving for him, I
suspect. He always pressed me to go a little bit slower.

My grandmother, too, was a lot of fun to be with. She was gentle and nice, and it was easier to do kid-type stuff with her than with
my grandfather, who tended to be more serious. I remember spending time playing with him, but usually he would be involved in more
mature matters, and I would lose interest quickly and wander off to
do something else.[7]

Kent grew up hearing the stories about his grandfather's immigration to
America, about Mr. Mac's having worked awhile as a cowboy to eke out a liveli-
hood. And, in addition to visiting the farm fairly often, Kent was part of the
Shamrock events that the family always participated in. There were the annual
grocer breakfasts held for customers and employees at the dairy. He remembered, from childhood, riding in the rodeo parade in a horse-drawn milk wagon
that has since been restored and used, by him and his children, in the annual St.
Patrick's Day parade in Phoenix. Most of his family memories involve various
holiday events, all centered in Tucson. For him, the company and the family
were tightly linked, and most people—Shamrock employees and members of

the McClelland and Parker families alike—assumed that Kent would eventually be joining the company. But for his part, Kent admittedly vacillated.

Kent McClelland

I didn't know that I *didn't* want to work for the company and I also didn't know that I *did*. What I did know was that I wanted to gain some other experience. I remember having all sorts of interesting fantasies about different possible lifestyles, different things I might want to do. For a long time I thought of becoming a doctor. In fact, when I left home for college, that's what I planned to study; I was going to be a premed student. But when I finally got down to the nitty-gritty of required course work, I found I didn't much care for it. I could handle it; I just didn't like it. I didn't like some of the early prerequisites of going into the medical field.

On the other hand, I was never interested in being an attorney or an accountant. Those professions never tweaked my interest. In fact, while in college I specifically stayed away from business subjects. My major ultimately was physics, and that's about as far removed as you can get from business. The hard sciences, generally speaking, do not lend themselves well to business, although ironically all my business school buddies had undergraduate degrees in engineering, physics, or chemistry. But that's what the business community was looking for—people who had a methodical, hard-science grasp of problem solving and could go on to understand the way businesses worked.

I went to college with no intention of focusing on business, however. I knew that I could probably pick that up along the way. In my first couple of years of college I didn't know what I wanted; then I took some physics courses and really liked the subject, so I stuck with it, finishing out with a physics major. At the end of four years I was toying with the idea of going on to get a master's degree and a Ph.D.

I attended college in Colorado Springs. When I graduated, I wasn't sure I wanted to start working on an advanced degree right away; instead, the time seemed right for me to finally try this business thing. And how better than to take a job with the family company. So from 1976 through part of 1978 I worked for Shamrock as a trainee, but even after that experience I still wasn't sure exactly what I wanted to do. I went off to Europe for six weeks, puttering around to get my head together. Finally I told Norman, "Well, I'm not really sure I want to go back to the company." He said, "Well, I'm not really sure that I want you to come back. Why don't you do something else for a while, and when you're serious about it, we'll talk. But it's not worthwhile for me— or for you either—to have you coming in and coming out, coming in and coming out."

So I took a job working on the night shift at Associated Grocers for the summer, loading shipping cases onto trucks from the loading dock at the freezer section of the warehouse. I ended up having saved some money and realizing that I really should go to business school. I had taken some basic business courses at Arizona State University, but they just didn't give me enough of what I needed. I knew that if I was going to get serious about business, I would have to go back to a more formal educational setting and fill in that gap . So I took the entrance exams for grad school and began sending out applications, then wound up working in Denver during the strike we had there. It was October 1978, and there was a need for people to come up from Arizona to support the Colorado division and keep the business going. I was one of those who came up for the second week of the strike, and I stayed on afterward, doing a number of different things.

In January of '79 I found myself working as the office manager, actually the accounting manager, which was something I was completely unqualified to do. I didn't have the training. United Food Service was a relatively small company by today's standards but big enough to require somebody pretty strong to make sure things didn't get lost in the shuffle, that accounts were reconciled on time and that bills and accounts were paid up on time. That experience convinced me more than anything that I needed to go back to school and really focus on business training.

So at the end of the summer I packed up and headed west, spending the next two years at UCLA. I graduated from the School of Business with a finance and marketing emphasis, and then I did what nobody at Shamrock expected me to do—most people assumed that I'd go off to business school and come right back. But I said, "No, I'm not coming right back, thank you very much. I'm going to go work for somebody else." I knew intuitively that there was a lot that I hadn't learned and couldn't learn if I was working in this company, because I was the boss's son and people wouldn't tell me. What I really felt was that if I was going to make mistakes, I wanted somebody else to have to pay for them rather than Shamrock.

More important, I guess, was that I wanted the opportunity to do something different, and to find out if I truly wanted to stay in the business world and, if so, was it the food-service and dairy business, or would some other type of business be more preferable? Since I had a background in finance, I took a job in the Los Angeles branch office of a small Canadian bank doing real estate construction finance. We were financing the building of warehouses and office towers, retail spaces, and some—very few—residential projects. It was a wonderful entrepreneurial company to work for, with good people, who knocked off a lot of my rough edges.

I had accepted a position with the bank in June, just before receiving my degree, but told them I wouldn't be able to report to work until sometime in September. Why? Because I was committed to going to Wales for the summer to work for a ship repairer. As one of the facilitators for a Young Presidents' Organization conference conducted at UCLA, I was introduced to this YPO fellow, a wild Welshman named Christopher Bailey who invited me and Celia to come over and work for his company. Each year he recruited interns for summer jobs and after getting to know me asked, "Why don't you come work for me this summer?" Celia and I were newlyweds then; we both made the trip, did some work for Bailey, and spent a wonderful summer in Wales. I came back reenergized and rejuvenated, ready to start my job at the bank. I worked there for the next three years.

By October of '81, interest rates had risen to 21½ or 22 percent, so for the first eighteen months that I worked for the bank we didn't do much selling. My job mostly was trying to devise ways to collect, to dispose of projects, to get permanent financing in place on projects. And during the last eighteen months we were able to sell a lot of projects. Even so, I knew then that this was just a temporary situation, three to five years at most, a way for me to get my feet wet in finance. In May of '84, when our first child was born, Celia and I decided it was time to move on. I left the bank and gave Norman a call. "I guess I'm ready to start back at Shamrock," I said. "What do you think would be a good spot for me?" He said, "Well, we're really in need of help in Denver, in the Colorado division." So that's where I went.

But when I got to Denver, they didn't know what to do with me, what title to give me or what area of responsibility I should cover. Norman and David finally decided that I should go to work in purchasing and accounting. "See what you can do there, see what you can do to improve the operation," they suggested. I didn't have a title or anything; I was just Kent McClelland.

The division had just made a deal to sell the old Mozer-Covillo warehouse over on Fortieth Avenue, and none of the officers were around. Norman wasn't there, Dave was out of town, and as they needed somebody to sign the papers to complete the sale, I was anointed. But in order to do what was needed, I had to be made an officer of the company, which explains why—seemingly overnight—I became a vice president.

It was one of the funniest experiences in my career. I had just arrived; nobody knew me from Adam—except that I was the owner's son who had worked for a bank. The announcement of my being named a vice president had just been distributed, and I was walking down the hall. Our national account manager, Bob Beake, a real jokester, came up to me and shook my hand earnestly, saying, "Congratulations, Kent. You really worked hard for it." Bob's a wonderful fellow with a marvelous sense of humor, and that's come back to haunt him—we've joked about it a number of times over the years.

At any rate, I became a VP, a VP of nothing, just a VP so I could sign some papers. Then for a couple of years I worked closely with Dave, who was truly my mentor and my professor. By 1986 he and Jeanne had decided to move back to Arizona, which is one of the things that keeps happening time and time again. None of our senior managers who went to Colorado ever wanted to stay there for an extended period of time because of the climate. I was the first one who really didn't mind it. I enjoyed it, in fact, and since Celia grew up in Denver, she already had a lot of friends and family there.[8]

The winter 1986 edition of *Shamrock News* carried the following item under the headline "Organization Announcement":

Over the many years that David B. Hall has been part of the Shamrock organization, he has had the privilege of announcing personnel promotions and corporate changes that have greatly benefited our company. The following announcement is the one of which he is the most proud, and the one which will insure the continued success of Shamrock Foods Company.

Effective October 1, 1986, the start of our new fiscal year, Shamrock's Board of Directors appointed Kent McClelland to serve as President and General Manager of the Colorado Foods Division. As President, Kent will have full responsibility for all operations, with all department managers reporting to him. Please join Dave in congratulating Kent, and share in his confidence that Kent will provide the leadership that is needed for our continued growth.[9]

The next "Organization Announcement" affecting Kent would be made by his father, confirming that on his return to Phoenix, in October 1992, he would become president and chief operating officer of Shamrock Foods Company as Norman assumed the dual role of chairman and chief executive officer. And Norman could point with pride to the fact that, from his base in Colorado, Kent "has been the force behind the quality initiative that is now a major part of our entire operation."[10]

By age thirty-eight, Kent had traveled a very long road.

Chapter Eleven

Wheels of Change

*K*ent McClelland was not alone in having begun his Shamrock career at the helm of a delivery route. From the company's earliest days, delivering product became the starting point for many a Shamrock employee who eventually achieved management status—men like Charlie Roberts, who rose to be vice president of personnel, for example. The job was never as simple as just learning to drive a truck or following a prescribed route; it represented the core of customer relations. For the deliveryman, known in the earliest days as the milkman, was the person who projected the Shamrock image of quality product and peerless service to the company's growing list of customers.

In a reflective "I Remember When" article for the *Shamrock News*, longtime employee Bill Hayden described the trials and tribulations of home delivery.

WILLIAM "BILL" HAYDEN
Longtime Shamrock employee

By 1949, routes were going to Benson, Bisbee, and Douglas. Back then, ice had to be shoveled on top of the loads to keep the milk cold while out making deliveries. Then there was the time a bunch of bottles were not completely filled, so a penny was taped onto the top of each bottle so as not to shortchange the customer.[1]

Carl Mrusek, who started with Shamrock in 1952 as a wholesale routeman, remembered how it was to make deliveries in a nonrefrigerated truck.

CARL MRUSEK
Retired Shamrock employee in Tucson

We would load up at 3:30 A.M. and go over to the ice house and ice the milk down. We had burlap bags and shovels, and we filled the bags with flaked ice and put them over the milk. We had cartons as well as glass bottles on our trucks at the time, but the cartons were waxed on the outside so the ice didn't bother them. But at the stores you had to get a mop and mop up the mess it made on the floors.[2]

Shortly before retiring as general manager of the dairy division in 1994, Derrell Fairfield paused to reflect on his early Shamrock career, which began in 1960, when, for six months, he was an independent distributor with his own territory. After that he joined the company as a supervisor.

DERRELL FAIRFIELD

I started back in the days when we worked six days a week, and if there was anything to do on Sunday, we did that too. We'd normally get to work around six or seven in the morning, and I would say that eighty percent of the time we'd still be there at six or seven at night. That kind of hard work is what grew the company.

We had the house count in Tucson, and at that time we knew we served a third of the houses with our home delivery. I don't mean that a third of the homes took home delivery; we, as Shamrock, served a third of the total homes in Tucson. There wasn't any street in town or a single block of a street where we didn't have a customer. It was a hardworking time but a friendly time. It was the era of everybody trusting the milkman.

When I had the route, I had better than sixty house keys on a key ring—so I could put milk in people's refrigerators when they weren't home. Many of my customers didn't have any idea how much milk they drank until I gave them a bill at the end of the month. When they got below six eggs, I'd put another dozen in there, and when their juice got halfway down, I'd put in another carton. I'd put everything right in the refrigerator, then rotate it around. They didn't realize how much milk or juice they were drinking, but people trusted me. It was a different era then. You knew all the kids' names, and as you walked down the street everybody would speak to you because you were the milkman.[3]

Another former routeman, Ossie Koepp, also had what he considered a unique relationship with his customers.

OSCAR "OSSIE" KOEPP, JR.
Retired home deliveryman in Tucson

On Christmas Eve, or a few days before, I would dress as Santa Claus and call on customers who had small children. I would do this during the dinner hour when the family was together. I would also present the smaller children with a gift of a quart of chocolate milk as a memento on their birthdays.[4]

Jack Underwood, who made a name for himself selling radio advertising before putting a lasting stamp on Shamrock as founding editor of *Shamrock News* in 1969, began his professional career as a Tucson newspaperman. He could remember that before World War II home delivery was basically the only way a retail customer could purchase milk. And since most people didn't have refrigeration, milk didn't keep too long at home, thus had to be brought to the doorstep daily.

JACK UNDERWOOD

Before the war, milk was delivered seven days a week, from 2 till 7 A.M., in pint- and quart-size glass bottles. With the war came gasoline and tire rationing and government regulations, so home delivery was divided into A and B routes. Each routeman delivered his A route on Monday, Wednesday, and Friday, his B route on Tuesday, Thursday, and Saturday. Milk was rationed, but with savvy foresight Shamrock acquired enough raw milk on contracts to service other competing dairies whose supply came up short.[5]

Jack had come to Tucson just out of high school, at the start of the Great Depression; unable to afford college, he took a job at Gambril's Market, which he called the first supermarket in town. It was located on North Fourth Avenue just above East Sixth Street.

JACK UNDERWOOD

Grocery stores were not a big outlet for dairy products then because people had home delivery, but we did have milk in the dairy case—in pint bottles and some quarts from Yale Dairy and a little bit from Shamrock. We also had an ice cream section that was just a little three-hole box by the cash register. People bought quarts or pints of ice cream because no one could afford a whole gallon at that time. Milk was twelve cents a quart; ice cream, twenty cents.[6]

John Harty was offered a route through northern Tucson when he applied for a job with Shamrock in 1948. "They didn't have any business in that area, out Oracle Road," he recalled, "but promised me that if I could develop a route there I could have a job. A lot of people were moving into that area, so I went to work. I was a retail routeman until we built a couple of routes in that area; then I was made a supervisor of the retail operation in Tucson, mainly running routes and training new people as the number of routes expanded."[7]

By the 1960s the structure of the American family began to change. Until then, typically, there was one car per household and one source of income. That was Dad, and he would take the family car in the morning, leaving Mom at home, so it was convenient to have goods and services come to her—laundry pickup and delivery, dry cleaning and, of course, milk. The difference between what a gallon of milk cost in a grocery store and what it cost home-delivered was sometimes only a penny, hardly enough to outweigh the convenience of having milk brought right to the doorstep.

F. Phillips Giltner, who became Shamrock's chief financial officer when Frances McClelland left that job in 1991, pointed out that when grocery stores started to grow and become supermarkets, they decided that a good way to pull customers into their stores was to use milk as a price leader.

F. PHILLIPS "PHIL" GILTNER
Chief Financial Officer of Shamrock Foods Company

The stores began selling milk for lower prices, so the difference between store purchase and home delivery got to be enormous. There were other changes, of course. People started eating out more often. Families bought second cars. Women went to work; they were no longer home during the day to greet the milkman. The company stayed close to the market on a daily basis so that it could react and adjust and figure out how to get more and more milk into people's refrigerators.[8]

Shamrock's home-delivery volume in Arizona reached its peak in the early 1960s with more than 150 routes statewide. But, Derrell Fairfield pointed out, "you could see the end of it when we went from a paper carton with a wax coating to one that was coated with plastic."[9]

DERRELL FAIRFIELD

Actually, wax-coated cartons were never very popular with consumers. We used to dip the cartons in wax, but no matter how careful we were, it was inevitable that a chunk of wax would get down into the milk now and then. And people would complain, "It tastes terrible, it's got a waxy taste to it." That's one reason they continued to favor home delivery in glass bottles. Another was that the milk seemed to stay colder in glass. But along about 1962, when the plastic-coated container (much cheaper than glass) was introduced and quickly won acceptance, and with the supermarkets promoting milk sales aggressively, you could see right away that it was going to be tough to continue competing with supermarkets on the home-delivery side.

Normal attrition helped reduce the number of routemen as our retail business began to shrink; we also hired some of the younger drivers who wanted to continue with us and trained them to start running wholesale routes. Our employee turnover rate has been traditionally low; one thing this company has always had is loyalty to its employees.[10]

In 1964, as a spur to sustaining home-delivery routes profitably, the first ten-quart plastic container came into use. It was essentially a plastic bag with a spigot, which when filled was inserted into an oblong corrugated carton that could be stored in nearly all home refrigerators. "This was quite a change in packaging," Jack Underwood noted. "It caused the wholesale market to start a price war on milk, but after a while the cost of using this package overcame its value, so it was deleted from our line of products."[11]

DERRELL FAIRFIELD

We were pioneers in what we called dispenser delivery. From attending industry conventions in different parts of the country, I could see that no one else was brave enough to take this step. We took the plunge because this large container, developed by the Scholle Company, didn't take up very much more room in a refrigerator than, say, three regular half-gallons. By being able to sell our customers the equivalent of five half-gallons with each ten-quart pack, we were ultimately able to convert to twice-a-week delivery.

I think that was really a milestone in the history of home delivery, because it allowed the routeman to service one set of customers Monday and Thursday, and another set Tuesday and Friday, still leaving him time to take on yet another full set of customers on Wednesday and Saturday. Our route average increased at least thirty percent, because routemen could be thirty percent more productive.

I think we set records at that time for the amount of milk delivered to the home. Having that little spigot was such a novelty, especially for children; they would run back and forth to the refrigerator, drinking our milk almost like water. People phoned us, wanting more and more delivered. It was quite an exciting time in my career.[12]

Another milestone was reached in 1966 with the distribution of refrigerated boxes, called Dairy Banks, to retail customers.

DERRELL FAIRFIELD

Each Dairy Bank held nine gallons of milk. We would leave this refrigerated box with the customer and deliver the product directly into it. This relieved the pressure for room in the household refrigerator and enabled us to serve more milk per delivery or again cut back on the frequency of the delivery we had previously made. The routeman's delivery costs could be further trimmed, and we could effectively hold our selling price down as low as possible to be more competitive with supermarkets. These programs were very successful through the 1960s.[13]

With the 1970s, when supermarkets started promoting dairy products on a daily basis, and the number of two-income families was rising steeply, the virtual demise of home-delivered milk seemed imminent. It was becoming harder than ever to compete with cut-rate pricing in the supermarkets and convenience stores. By 1980, Shamrock's retail routes had been reduced in number to only thirty, and the emphasis had shifted to wholesale delivery, traditionally the most daunting market.

DERRELL FAIRFIELD

We decided that our best approach to growing the wholesale business was to lower our price to the stores—to get it so low, in fact, that unlike California, where most major supermarket chains had their own dairy operations, it would not be feasible for stores to spend capital asset money to build dairy plants when they could buy

157

milk from an existing dairy so competitively. But to reduce the selling price we had to reduce our costs.

At that time all of the stores, even the supermarkets, were being served by a regular wholesale truck and given service. Routemen would go into the supermarkets, even the big chains, and inventory the dairy case, go back out to the truck and wheel the milk in. The same routemen would have to return maybe three times a day and pull this milk up, face it around, and do everything else.[14]

Louis "Chubby" Frede, who went to work for Shamrock in 1947, later remembered how he would service one of his very special wholesale customers in Tucson.

LOUIS "CHUBBY" FREDE
Retired wholesale delivery employee in Tucson

I had only seven stops, including the Goodman store. I would stop there and load them up with milk and other products, then I would go and deliver other stops. When I was done, I would return to Goodman's store and see if they needed anything else. Sometimes I'd even go back after dinner to check on what they might need. Goodman's slogan was, "We take the hopping out of shopping." I sure did the hopping for them.[15]

Derrell Fairfield said he could remember another Tucson-based routeman who had even fewer customers to service than "Chubby" Frede. He would deliver a load of milk to one supermarket and continue on, delivering to another. Then he would spend the rest of the day taking care of the milk he had put into each location.

DERRELL FAIRFIELD

Here was one man whose entire job consisted of going to just two supermarkets every day, and we could see that this was a very expensive delivery method. Out of this realization came our concept of express delivery, van delivery, drop shipment—call it what you will. We were determined to convince store managers that they had personnel under their own roofs who could monitor the milk supply and display a lot less expensively than if our route-men did it, going back and back and back to each store.

In other words, we could lower our wholesale price, creating a savings, if the stores would take care of the milk themselves. We would continue to help them with their ordering, of course. In response, stores started calling in orders themselves instead of our having to go out and take the inventory and write the orders for them. As far as I know, we were among the first dairies in the country to adopt this strategy.[16]

Norman concurred that Shamrock "had been on the leading edge of inno-vation in adopting a truck-and-trailer delivery system and committing to extremely competitive drop-shipment store pricing. This innovation led to numerous plant, warehouse, and delivery incentive schemes in the dairy and foods divisions, because of the emphasis on larger volumes per man and per truck, which in turn has led to superior productivity. Other competi-tors have sold out or ceased operations over the years due to this highly competitive market."[17]

The pricing of milk to wholesale customers has depended in large part on geography as well as refrigerated trucks. The farther milk has to be transport-ed, the longer it takes to reach market shelves and the shorter its ultimate shelf life will be. In addition, observed Phil Giltner, "the weight of the product is such that it's feasible to transport it only so far. After all, you're mainly transporting water; there is an awful lot of fluid content in milk. Thus there is a geographical range that we can serve profitably, and it would end somewhere out there around the borders of Arizona, though there are some exceptions."[18]

Dave Hall pointed out that because Arizona summer temperatures are so high, Shamrock trailers traditionally had more insulation than those in most other areas.

DAVE HALL

We bought the biggest Thermo King, the power unit for refrigeration, that we could buy so that we could hold the temperature no matter what the weather was. Crossing the desert you could have 140-degree ambient temperatures on that road. I remember what it was like in the summer for some of the guys who worked for the transport company. In the days before the cabs were refrigerated along with the trailers, our drivers' feet would swell because the floorboards would get so hot. At the end of a trip from Yuma to Phoenix, they would hardly be able to get their shoes off. It's unimaginable how hot that desert is. Summer heat also affects milk production, often creating product shortages. When it's very, very hot here, milk production per cow falls off precipitously. And then when school starts up again and we get a lot of school business, if it's still very, very hot we will sometimes be in short supply and have to buy milk in Utah or California and bring it in. We can't afford to lose customers.[19]

It was in 1951 that Shamrock Dairy purchased its first refrigerated truck, one in which ice was no longer needed. "It had a good impact on quality of product," recalled Milt Sivesind. "Trucks were heavier, larger, and hauled more product and a larger variety of products to sell. Routemen could hold product over to the next day within their trucks and did not need to check in completely every night."[20] This was the beginning of what ultimately became a fully refrigerated fleet.

Don Van Wormer remembers a time, early in his Arizona Frozen Foods career, when loads would be sent out in small trucks in the morning and more loads would be sent out in the afternoon, also in small trucks. The trucks hauling dry product were also equipped to transport frozen foods.

DON VAN WORMER

At one time we used panel trucks to deliver food to the Biltmore Hotel, which was our largest single food-service account way back in the sixties. They demanded two deliveries a day—dry food in the morning, frozen food in the afternoon, or vice versa. So you'd load a little panel truck up with dry food and take it out in the morning, and in the afternoon your driver would come back and get another load—this time of frozen food—and take it back. Same driver, same little truck. Now, semis are used to deliver dry, refrigerated, and frozen—all on one truck.[21]

Trucks and the refinement of the distribution system were largely responsible for sustaining Shamrock's extraordinary growth, as the company shifted from fifteen-foot panel trucks to twenty-four-foot combo trucks, each with both a high- and low-temperature compartment that enabled it to carry milk and ice cream at the same time. The first express routes had twenty-four-foot trailers, which were replaced by trailers more than double their size by 1980. Improving the design and carrying power of delivery vehicles undoubtedly facilitated further growth, but Don Van Wormer credits another form of technology with a large measure of Shamrock's success: "When we first started, we didn't have computers, but without them we never would have experienced the growth we had. For, ultimately, computers increased our efficiency in controlling inventory as well as monitoring receivables and payables—in fact, everything."[22]

"Progress in action has been the hallmark of Shamrock from the beginning," wrote Bill Hayden in an article in *Shamrock News*. "Much of the work was still being done by hand as the '60s made their debut."[23]

BILL HAYDEN

The cases were filled, stacked, and loaded into the trucks with a grunt and groan until 1962 when air-operated stackers were installed, helping to lighten the load. On the other hand, before the proliferation of computers the drivers, when making a delivery, would fill out an order form for the wholesale customers' next delivery. This was then given to the Cold Room, which would put up the order, making any required changes. The Cold Room then gave one copy back to the driver and the other to the Accounting Department, which then billed the customer. Simple, neat, and effective—and most surprising of all, done on pencil power....

Confusing to me were the keypunch cards that those first computers used. All information was punched into a card in a form typed onto a card in type only a computer could figure out. All the cards were ingested by the computer, which would sort it all out and print out the reams of paperwork needed to feed a growing company. Of course, now the computer is smart enough to watch all the terminals and ingest the information directly while printing out those reams of paper. It took until 1984 for the Dairy Division to get away from keypunch. By the way, those cards made for great scratch paper.[24]

Bob Gray, who was in charge of operations in the Arizona Foods Division for fifteen years ending with Duane Lawson's arrival in 1993, described what a typical day of delivery might be at that time.

Robert "Bob" Gray
Retired Operations Manager of Arizona Foods Division

First, there were deadlines. For salesmen in the Phoenix area it was 6:00 P.M.; in areas beyond a fifty-mile radius of the metropolitan area, with the exception of Tucson and Prescott, it would be three hours earlier. At any rate, by six o'clock salesmen using laptop computers and modems had input their orders into computers installed along one wall of the warehouse. After the orders were confirmed and any needed substitutions made, the information was downloaded and plugged into the mainframe. At 6:00 P.M., all the orders were transmitted to the dispatcher. The salespeople could be out there till six o'clock selling, if that's what was required.

Between 6:00 and 6:30 P.M. we would start loading the trucks. The first one would leave at about 9:30, heading for El Paso, Texas, which was 450 miles away, our farthest point. Then our fresh order, or fresh express, would take over: live people talking to live people. It was called fresh but was primarily produce, and we'd take those orders until 11:00 or 11:30 at night, but even if customers called after that, we'd still take orders. We were not going to tell them no.

Between 4:30 and 5:00 in the morning, those trucks would all depart—we started out with two and wound up with twelve—heading for metro Phoenix and the major resorts, big places with a lot of volume. Most of the trucks would be back in sometime between 9:30 and 11:30. Half of them would be loaded up again and sent back out, sometimes to the same customers—maybe they forgot something or decided they wanted something more. A lot of those nice resorts weren't built with very much storage space.

Then we would also do what were called relays, same-day orders where the customer or the salesperson calls in for something needed right away. Maybe a mistake was made when the order was placed or a party had been overlooked on the schedule. Or maybe it was our fault because we didn't have a product on hand when the customer wanted it. No matter. We'd load it on one of these same trucks; we've even been known to fly things to El Paso.[25]

Dave Hall pointed out that this level of service is part of what has separated Shamrock from its competitors, the majority of whom have never been so consistently responsive to customer needs.

DAVE HALL

Most of our customers don't have big warehouses that would allow them to order a week in advance. They usually order for next-day delivery or for even that same day, and if they order it, we know they need it. So we take care of them, which helps create a lasting bond.

I think this kind of service goes back to the dairy's early success, when people were moving to Arizona and the area was growing so much. Everybody had heard of Borden's and Carnation, Meadow Gold, Foremost and Arden, but they had never heard of Shamrock. So we had to do things a little differently, give them a little more attention. That's how we built our reputation, by delivering superlative service. I think it's one reason we're still in business, and why a lot of companies have gone *out* of business, why we do so much volume in the food-service area, why we do much more than our next two nearest competitors combined.[26]

Giving customers extra consideration in time, effort, and price has paid off handsomely for Shamrock, boosting revenues as well as market share. "You'd like to have one stated delivery system, but it just isn't possible," Dave insisted. "A lot of companies do that, but they don't have the market share or dominate the market as we do."[27] To maintain this dominance means never saying no.

BOB GRAY

Although weekends are quiet, we would have a small receiving crew on hand every Saturday. We'd really be shut down on Sunday until late in the afternoon, but there'd be a supervisor in each area—frozen, refrigerated, and dry. They'd rotate on beeper from weekend to weekend. So if a customer happened to call in at ten o'clock Friday night or seven o'clock Sunday morning, a supervisor would get beeped. He would come down here, assemble the order and call a driver in, if it was necessary or if the order was big enough, or he would take care of the delivery himself. He was authorized to go anyplace in the state, putting orders on buses or airplanes or running them in cars. We'd want him to do whatever it took to get orders to customers.[28]

Shamrock also maintained a series of short-order weekday noon runs to Las Vegas, particularly for major accounts like Perkins and Sizzler. Plus there were always special nighttime deliveries—to Las Vegas customers, certainly, and also to those in Phoenix. None of these ever interfered with normal daytime deliveries.

BOB GRAY

A truck would leave here about eight o'clock at night and get to Vegas about midnight or one o'clock, and the driver would start unloading. He'd carry keys, let himself in, and immediately disarm the alarm system. Sometimes he'd forget, of course, and the police would show up.[29]

Personal service, from Shamrock right to the customers' shelves and refrigerators—that's been a Shamrock hallmark from the start. For many of its wholesale customers, a relationship exists with the driver that rivals the rapport the housewife had with the milkman during the glory days of home delivery. Special deliveries are made on demand, but regular runs generally occur between 6 A.M. and 8 A.M., averaging anywhere from sixty-five to ninety truck deliveries a day and up to four hundred a week.

Shamrock's fleet by the mid-'80s included eighteen-foot trucks and forty-foot trailers, and every vehicle was refrigerated—frozen and refrigerated. Fully half of the vehicles were built with separate compartments for frozen, refrigerated, and dry product, each with movable shelves for greater loading and unloading flexibility. Bob Gromko, who was involved in operations in the dairy division from the time he joined Shamrock in 1978, defined the company's normal over-the-road truck as a forty-foot van, a tractor with a forty-foot trailer. But, he added, "we've had some twenty-seven-foot vans that could be run as doubles—one tractor pulling two twenty-seven-foot trailers."[30] He also pointed out that a twenty-seven-foot trailer could be operated more efficiently than a forty-footer.

ROBERT "BOB" GROMKO
Vice President of Dairy Operations

Picture backing a forty-foot trailer into a convenience store to make a delivery, and then picture a twenty-seven-foot trailer. With the kind of service we provide to our convenience-store customers, a twenty-seven-foot trailer holds more than enough milk than would be needed. So in that situation there's no advantage to having a longer trailer. Of course, we do have some solo trucks that are a little smaller, either eighteen or twenty feet. And then we go all the way down to panel-truck size, as there is still a little bit of door-to-door retail milk delivery.[31]

BOB GRAY

We always took a lot of pride in the way we delivered ice cream. Our vehicles were equipped to hold it, but we'd go a step further and put it into insulated containers that held dry ice, ensuring that the ice cream was kept frozen hard. That way we could make sure the ice cream got where it was going in A-1 condition. We worked real hard to get everything right the first time.[32]

Dave Hall pointed out that keeping products like ice cream frozen hard was essential in combating Arizona's temperature and altitude extremes.

DAVE HALL

If your load isn't frozen hard as you head for Flagstaff, whose elevation is over seven thousand feet, for example, everything will expand. With ice cream, if it's not frozen hard enough, the lids will come off the containers and it'll expand a great deal, since the air inside the product has less pressure on it due to the altitude.[33]

In the long run, the customer doesn't care about the problems of packing and delivery. He wants his product to arrive when he needs it and in good condition. "When all is said and done," Dave concluded, "the only thing you have is your customers, and when you give them the service they need, they always appreciate it."[34] And Kent McClelland echoed these sentiments, stressing that Shamrock was continually looking at ways to serve customers more effectively—and also striving to make its distribution of product more cost effective.

KENT McCLELLAND

We used to run everything out of these big warehouses, and the driver would take it to the end of the earth in delivery and then come home. Now we're more likely to take a two-trailer rig to a point where it's then split up and taken by other drivers for delivery. It's what is called a shuttle program, a kind of relay, and that's a departure from what we've done in the past. We're finding now that the shuttle program works effectively for long hauls, but even for short distances—from Phoenix to Tucson—it can work pretty well if it's properly planned.

Over time, I think back-hauls are going to become much more the way of getting product into our warehouse than they have been in the past, particularly as we expand into southern California. Right now, if we hop over the hill into San Bernardino, we are at a point where we can pick up products that we need for our warehouse and back-haul it to Phoenix. I think that for the kind of business we're doing today, we can handle a 450-mile radius without significantly altering the level of service to our customers.[35]

Kent pointed out that Los Angeles fell into the 450-mile range. Would the LA market ever be a target? "It may be, or it may not be," he said cryptically. "At this time, we certainly are eying it carefully."[36]

Chapter Twelve

Enjoying Success,
Enduring Adversity

The years between the early seventies and the early eighties were marked by continued expansion for Shamrock—in Colorado as well as Arizona, in food service as well as milk production and distribution. Following the Inland Frosted Foods acquisition in 1970 and the Meadow Gold purchase the following year, the decade saw Shamrock establishing its own meat department (1971), merging United Food Service into Inland Frosted Foods (1975), acquiring the Colorado-based Continental Food Service (1978) and the Berry-Losee Food Equipment and Supply Company (1980), and absorbing the Arizona assets of Romney Produce Company (1982). In 1983, the year the new Colorado warehouse finally opened—tripling the capacity of its predecessor—United Food Service of Colorado became known officially as Shamrock Foods.

The meat manufacturing facility was one of the Arizona Frozen Foods properties acquired by Shamrock. Located on McDowell Road in Phoenix, it had been Arizona's first state-inspected meat plant. In 1972 Shamrock applied for a federal meat-inspection permit, and the plant was renovated and updated according to federal specifications. A year later Shamrock won approval for federal meat inspection, enabling the plant to ship product out of state and also to participate in federal distribution within the Arizona borders. In October 1979 the meat manufacturing plant began serving the foods company in

Colorado, periodically shipping to it a full line of patties and ground beef from Phoenix. Three years later the plant had broadened its focus to provide Shamrock's customer base with special cuts of meat, ranging from boneless lamb chops to all varieties of steak cuts.

It was through Inland-United's skillful intercession that Shamrock was able to purchase the Denver branch of Continental Food Service. Established as a coffee company in 1915, Continental had expanded its capacity over the years to include other food items and do business countrywide. Because the Continental purchase did not include a building, the company's inventory had to be shoehorned into the Inland-United warehouse. Through this acquisition, however, the Shamrock organization was able to achieve high ranking among Colorado's prominent beverage distributors.

During the decade ending in 1983, the year Gerry Gulick was just beginning his career as controller for the Arizona Foods Division, Shamrock's food-service sales climbed to more than $100 million. In another company, such extraordinary growth might have been accompanied by internal stress and turmoil plus frequent changes at the top, but food-service industry insiders proclaimed a minor miracle the fact that Shamrock managed to maintain family-style pride and dedication throughout its work force, plus the steady course set by its management. One reason for this stability may have been the incentive programs that kept Shamrock employees goal oriented and motivated.

Throughout the course of its history, the company had pioneered various motivational rewards for performance, including bonus pools for workers that reduced overtime and overhead, incentive programs for individual workers who devised cost- or time-saving techniques, and rewards for managers who achieved or exceeded the business objectives they set. And through the years Shamrock had added exponentially to its customer base, beginning with Mr. Mac and door-to-door delivery and culminating in the large-scale servicing of grocery stores, food chains, restaurants, fast-food outlets, hotels, hospitals, schools, airlines and military installations: two hundred dairy items and more than nine thousand food items.

With the absorption of the Berry-Losee Food Equipment & Supply Company, Shamrock was suddenly able to offer customers a range of design services and food and facility equipment lines plus a full line of kitchen, table-top, and restaurant supply items. Founded in 1947, Berry-Losee had become Arizona's largest commercial firm of its kind thirty-five years later. At the time it was acquired by Shamrock, it was selling more than five thousand items ranging from teaspoons and salt and pepper shakers to chandeliers and complete commercial kitchens. It catered to such commercial food establishments as restaurants, schools, hotels, and hospitals, and provided complete contract interior design packages and commercial kitchen installations.

The sale to Shamrock was made by Lowell and Kent Berry, who had attained full ownership of the company in 1972. The Berry brothers purchased it so they could become business partners at last, but ultimately decided to sell when they realized that, try as they might, they could not make it profitable. Lowell had been president of the Black and Ryan Appliance Company, a large wholesale appliance company that served Arizona, while Kent was previously with Dog House Restaurants and Food Makers.

By 1982, a new tabletop and equipment showroom was completed in Shamrock's Phoenix food-service warehouse on West Encanto Boulevard: 2,300 square feet of floor space with the capacity for displaying more than a hundred light and heavy equipment items and about four thousand small tabletop wares. Included in the displays were large numbers of china, glassware and flatware items, slicers, butcher knives, meat market accessories, trays of all sizes, popcorn machines, microwave ovens, ranges, grills, and warming ovens. All of these items were readily available to both large and small clients: hospital kitchens, school cafeterias, military mess facilities, and even large commercial restaurants. Additionally, one room was devoted exclusively to paper products, disposables, and chemicals. Through the staffing of this new facility, Shamrock developed the ability to turn a completely empty space into a fully equipped, completely furnished snack bar, restaurant, or bakery that could then be supplied contin-ually by the Institutional Foods Division.

The acquisition of Romney Produce made Shamrock a full-line food-service company at last and also the ninth largest food-service operation in the country, serving both Colorado and Arizona. Additionally, it brought another new product line to Shamrock's Phoenix-based food-service division. Romney, a fifty-six-year-old company with an excellent reputation, was headquartered in Phoenix with a branch in Tucson. The transfer of equipment and inventory was managed by manpower from both the Shamrock dairy and foods divisions.

On January 2, 1983, salespeople, data-processing personnel, and operations employees gathered to watch the night warehouse crew place the first loads of regular Shamrock merchandise on trucks along with some 150 items of fresh Romney produce. It would be a scramble for a while as the company learned to handle, store, merchandise, and deliver the new product, but a large measure of growth experienced by the Arizona Foods Division would be attributed to the importance of produce. And with the addition of Gene Romney, Lavar West, and Bill Hansen to the Shamrock team—and Bill Hansen's management of the innovative Shamrock Fresh Express customery delivery service—the company quickly attained the number-one position in fresh produce in the greater Phoenix market.

With Shamrock's move into fresh produce came its affiliation with Markon, a buying cooperative that started out small but grew to be one of the biggest food-service buying cooperatives in America. Dave Hall described working with Markon as a way to assure even the smallest producers of receiving prompt payment and also of eliminating brokers, the perennial middlemen. By arrangement, Markon would pay the bills and Shamrock would pay Markon. The single most important advantage offered by Markon has been having the clout to deliver top-quality produce on demand.

DAVE HALL

Through Markon, we can supply customers with produce in whatever form they wish. Lettuce, for example, doesn't come just in cases. It's available three to a pack, or individually packed or even cored, if that's the way a customer wants it. That's the key: Produce is delivered the way *our* customer wants it—as opposed to the house-wife feeling her way through a supermarket display of avocados, for example, and saying, "I think that's a good one." Chefs in restaurant, hotel, or resort kitchens know exactly what they want, and what that is, basically, is top-quality goods on demand, 365 days a year. Prices may fluctuate, but for these special customers quality and packaging are more important considerations.

Many people don't realize that food service often pays more than retail. We're willing to pay more to get what we want, to satisfy our customers. It's up to Markon to obtain the product from wherever it might be available. Pricing may be more competitive in food service, but it might not be cheaper than retail. When quality produce is at its peak, the price may be low because growing conditions are choice. But when it's raining and the lettuce comes up muddy, the price goes sky high, yet we can still get the very best of whatever is available.

If a five-star resort wants fresh raspberries in the middle of winter, that's our problem, and that's when Markon becomes invaluable. If Markon says the raspberries have to be flown in from Chile or New Zealand, we have to agree to it—because our customer wants them. Markon has been as important to us in produce as Frosty Acres has been in frozen foods.[1]

Nineteen eighty-two was not only the year Shamrock embraced fresh produce but also when the lineup of products included the common item of water. It was pumped from company wells near the Catalina foothills and, at the outset, stored there in 2,500-gallon tanks before processing. The company claimed its water was so superior that it could be used anywhere in the house—as distilled water, as drinking water, and even as water for preparing baby formula. Besides adding another commodity, the merchandising of water was another way of utilizing Shamrock's vast transport and servicing system to the fullest. Earlier, water had been used in the manufacture of fruit drinks and as the liquid needed to make 100 percent orange juice from concentrate. But then, having the potential to package and sell bottled drinking water, Shamrock decided to share in that growing market. To compete for business, it was essential to have the highest quality product.

The first step in this direction was to pump water from the deepest wells, then send it through a sand filter to remove organic matter. Still another process, demineralization, removed most of the sodium and led to the final step of reverse osmosis and deionization to remove virtually all undesirable elements. Shamrock added another process known as ultraviolet sterilization to purify the water completely so that it met all federal, state, and local standards. It was now ready for bottling in gallon or ten-quart handy-top dispensers.

Another Shamrock milestone was reached when, approaching its golden anniversary, it received an invitation to join Master Dairies, Inc., a national association of privately owned dairies. The organization had been conceived by two independents, Purity Dairy in Nashville and Pine State Dairy in Raleigh, North Carolina. Their owners, dismayed that there was no trade association for their industry, had decided that since the two dairies were not competing with each other, they should get together and explore the possible advantages of collective buying without compromising any facet of their marketing image or individuality. The idea caught on.

By 1965, Master Dairies comprised five large independents and had developed a plan to add approximately one additional member each year. With Shamrock's affiliation in 1971, the association numbered eleven constitutent companies made up of twenty processing plants from coast to coast. The members at that time represented combined sales of approximately $225 million, and the buying corporation was owned equally by its partners, each of whom was allotted one seat on the board.

According to its charter, the overall purpose of Master Dairies, Inc., was to build an organization that would do for the member companies whatever "would help them to be more competitive in the marketplace with their national competition."[2] By the time Shamrock became affiliated, this objective was a virtual accomplishment, rewarding its constituents with the fruits of group purchasing plus the sharing of ideas and technical knowledge in all phases of dairy operation. Shamrock's management felt that membership in an exclusive group devoted to achieving mutual benefits and keeping the dairy industry abreast of the latest business and technical advances lent prestige and added another dimension to its own sales marketing efforts.

In March 1981, an engraved plaque was presented to Paul Dew of Shamrock Dairy in recognition of his ten years' service as a director of Master Dairies, Inc. At that time he was relinquishing his position on the Master Dairies board because of his imminent retirement from Shamrock as a senior vice president of the dairy division. He had joined the company in 1969, and ended his career as a senior vice president in both the Tucson and Phoenix dairy divisions. Derrell Fairfield, the dairy division general manager, was elected to replace him on a Master Dairies board that by then represented thirty affiliates.

As a group, representatives of these independent dairies periodically taste-tested and compared their output for flavor and texture, gleaning constructive ideas and positive suggestions from such exercises. The dairies also shared information regarding successful methods of dairy accounting, data processing, and plant maintenance as well as product quality control.

Early in 1983, Derrell looked back favorably on twelve years of Shamrock's affiliation with the organization:

DERRELL FAIRFIELD

Our affiliation with Master Dairies gives us the buying power
of a Carnation, a Borden's, or Beatrice Foods....It gives us the
opportunity to purchase in volume. All of our invoices are paid

through Master Dairies, which negotiates the price for us and puts us in a very competitive position with the rest of them. At present, for example, we are collectively the largest paperboard purchaser in the United States. We are actually using more paper cartons than any other single purchaser. Along with the buying power we also have an exchange of ideas.

When Shamrock put the new blow-mold plastic bottle facility into operation, we did not have to go out and negotiate a price for the resin from which our bottles are made. We told the various companies that called us to contact the executive director of Master Dairies in Indianapolis, and he would decide whom we would purchase from. We did not have to offend anyone.

We have one man who holds the power of fifteen dairies. It's a tremendous edge we have over our competitors, and I think it is something that will be ongoing. The beautiful part is that we can exchange ideas without any fear of collusion or anything like that because they won't allow anyone to overlap into someone else's territory.[3]

A blow mold is a processing machine that transforms plastic resin into a plastic container. When Shamrock adopted this process early in 1983 so it could begin manufacturing its own plastic containers, a new room and a new dock had to be built, and electrical and air-conditioning services had to be installed along with chillers, air compressors, a resin silo, a bottle conveyor plus the blow molds themselves.

Developing the capacity to blow-mold its own plastic bottles, which the company had been considering since 1980, had become a serious objective by 1982 when Shamrock learned that one of its competitors planned to install such an operation in-house. Five months and about $1 million later, a new structure had been completed and the equipment was ready for start-up.

It had been determined that because a portion of the existing case dock could be enclosed, the need to construct a new and costly building to house the equipment could be averted. To compensate for the loss of space, the engineering and maintenance department constructed an addition on the west side of the existing dock. Shamrock's own construction crew erected the new case dock and also put the resin tower in place. Its capacity was 80,000 pounds, and the Shamrock operation would require 45,000 pounds of resin each week.

A giant crane plus heavy-duty supporting equipment had to be called in when the two Uniloy blow-molding machines arrived and the riggers were ready to remove them from the flatbed trucks. Cranes were also used to lift a twenty-ton chiller to the roof along with air conditioners and an air compressor. A conveyor system designed to accommodate 1,800 plastic bottles was erected by Automatic Inspection Systems. Regrind equipment was installed as well as trimmers, cooling beds, and resin bins. To handle the additional demand for power, it was necessary to install a new 4,000-amp electrical system.

After the blow-molding operation had been running about a year, a resin blender was installed. It blended the virgin material with the regrind in proper proportions so the resin was always uniform and the very best bottle could be produced. By using reground resin, waste could be reduced to the vanishing point.

In 1981, Shamrock received the pearl of national recognition when it was spotlighted as "a Great Distributor Organization" by *Institutional Distribution* magazine. That highly respected national trade publication devoted nearly all of its June issue to a review of Shamrock achievements. Editor in Chief Robert Civin introduced the issue with an editorial headlined "Success Story."

ROBERT CIVIN
Former editor in chief of Institutional Distribution magazine

Both United Food Service in Denver and Shamrock Institutional Foods in Phoenix are little over a decade old. Yet each is doing close to $60 million in annual volume. But to measure the achievement of these companies solely in terms of dollar sales tells only part of the story....Shamrock and United Food Service have backed their wide product capabilities with two of the best-trained sales forces in the industry. They have motivated their people through outstanding management-by-objective programs and by a variety of incentives in key sales and operational areas. The result has been extraordinarily high levels of service to their operator customers. Service to the operator is, of course, the ultimate objective. Because they have been so successful in training and motivating their people, the two Shamrock food-service distribution affiliates provide service at levels that are well above industry norms....

It is the sum of these achievements, made in what is a startlingly short period of time, that has led to the rapid rise of Shamrock Institutional Foods and United Food Service in food-service distribution. It is why they can truly be called Great Distributor Organizations.[4]

In their lead article, "The Company of Differences," the magazine's editors pointed out that Shamrock had "distinguished itself as a professional with a high degree of orientation toward its customers. Today, Shamrock Foods Company is still the leading dairy in Arizona. But it is also much more. The past decade has seen the company launch a full-scale drive into food-service distribution which has propelled it into the top ranks of this industry."[5]

The article pointed out further that Shamrock's high degree of customer service was made possible by a combination of financial control systems, internal incentives, and training programs, many of which were unique in the food-service distribution industry. Incentives in all programs, the article noted, increased productivity beyond industry norms. And this increase was reflected in economies that could be passed on to customers in addition to helping the company increase profitability.

In article after article, thirteen in all, the magazine explained in detail the means by which the institutional foods organization under the Shamrock banner in Arizona and Colorado had attained a high degree of efficiency and the wide acceptance of its products and methods. That issue of *Institutional Distribution* represented the highest recognition Shamrock and its components had received to date. As nothing else could have done, it placed the company in the limelight within its own industry and was the highlight of a year that also saw negative forces at work. These forces had already succeeded in compromising company morale and embroiling its management in long-drawn-out, dispiriting litigation.

In February 1972 Shamrock received a subpoena requesting that it furnish certain information to the federal government, and two years later class-action suits were filed against Shamrock and three other Arizona dairies—Borden, Carnation, and Foremost-McKesson—on behalf of consumers. Later, the case was widened to include charges that nine retail food chains were similarly engaged in fixing the retail price of milk.

NORMAN MCCLELLAND

There are actually two stories. One of them involved practices that got started back in our early days when school boards would allocate business based upon community service. As often happened, certainly at Shamrock, some company employees might have been board members, and they could be expected to say, "Well, we think the boss should have some of the business."

Over time, as the dairy industry grew and that sort of practice continued, there was a certain amount of questionable allocation, particularly of school business. We got into trouble with the federal government over that, so we had to pay a fine on that part of our business. As to the other indictment, which included the allegation of collusion with grocery stores in setting milk prices outside of the stores, we were never involved in that.[6]

The class-action suit alleged that the dairies and the retailers had determined what the price of milk would be for home delivery versus that which could be obtained in stores. "If you knew the grocers," Norman observed, "you'd know things didn't work that way. The stores were so competitive. One would drop prices, another would do something else. Collusion just wasn't possible."[7] Shamrock immediately turned the case over to its legal adviser, John Christian of Jennings, Strouss & Salmon. "Until his death in 1970, Riney Salmon had been our contact on all legal matters," said Norman. "John Christian followed in Riney's footsteps. They and their colleagues in the firm have offered consistently sound legal advice but have also done so in a manner consistent with the ethical values of our company."[8]

Norman initially pleaded not guilty to the antitrust allegations, but with mixed emotions he ultimately changed his plea to nolo contendere ("I do not wish to contend"), a type of plea that subjected him to possible conviction but with no need for an admission of guilt. At that time, he said, it seemed that there was no other plea he could make. "My attorneys were authorized to request a modification of the indictment to allege only the violation in relationship to the schools and to state that I was willing to plead guilty to that charge," Norman noted in his statement to the court. "I was advised [that] the Justice Department, as a matter of policy, would not change an antitrust indictment. However, I know in my own heart that I was innocent of the other things with which I was charged and that no one was injured by my activities."[9]

The antitrust allegations were not only distressing but deeply embarrassing to Norman, as Shamrock's president, because of the way the charges of wrongdoing affected his employees as well as the retail chains that were Shamrock customers.

NORMAN MCCLELLAND

In one phase of the litigation, regarding bids for local school districts and other government agencies, the dairy industry had made some mistakes. For example, a cooperative industry plan which started as an honest effort to benefit school customers by rear-ranging delivery routes ended up as an activity that violated antitrust regulations. Shamrock admitted these mistakes and paid the price, settling for $835,000. Even these institutional customers, however, benefited from lower milk prices than their counterparts in neighboring states. By 1979 all claims against Shamrock had been cleared up—except the consumer class action.[10]

Borden, Carnation, and Foremost-McKesson, as divisions of giant national corporations, decided against sustaining the costly legal procedures that would have ensued had they contested the allegations. So instead of continuing the fight, each paid their portion of the $4.075 million penalty as an out-of-court settlement of the class action. But Shamrock stood firm. The company's total net worth at the time was $4,205,897; the plaintiffs' demand from Shamrock, because of its market share, totaled well over $3 million. So not only was the company not interested in settling the lawsuit as the others had done, it could have risked financial ruin if it had tried to do so.

More important, said Norman, the company "felt that the consumer class-action lawsuit had no basis in fact because there were no antitrust violations in the consumer lawsuit, and Arizona consumers were, had been, and continued enjoying milk at prices less than consumers in other states."[11]

People, then, may have been surprised to learn that milk prices to schools in Arizona were consistently and substantially lower than those in neighboring states—New Mexico and California, for example. At the same time, Shamrock paid more for milk before processing it than dairies paid in those contiguous states, the result in part of Shamrock's aggressive efforts, over the years, to reduce the cost of processing and delivering milk. Together with a highly competitive grocery marketing system, Shamrock had achieved virtually the narrowest spread in the country between the cost of milk to the dairies and the price to the consumer.

NORMAN MCCLELLAND

The government has consistently said in this action that it was immaterial whether prices were higher, lower, or the same as they otherwise would have been. A violation of the antitrust laws is a violation without regard to whether there was resulting change in what consumers paid. This my lawyers have clearly advised me is the law and I understand it to be. Thus even though the schools received a fair price, I am still guilty in relationship to them.[12]

Norman concluded his courtroom statement with a proposal that, as community service, he be allowed to lend assistance to Second Harvest, a new program begun in Maricopa County to provide food-bank services to the poor and needy. For Norman this would be one more voluntary undertaking in a lifetime of community service. A decade later he would take some satisfaction from the fact that none of the giant dairy companies that were Shamrock's competitors named in the lawsuit remained in business in Arizona.

In May 1987 Norman announced to Shamrock employees that "the company is about to settle an important legal case involving unfair and unwarranted charges of price fixing. We feel we have been totally vindicated. The settlement came after a court ruling which the attorney general labeled in a news release as 'unfavorable' to his case. The heart of that ruling was that after thirteen long years of floundering, the plaintiffs were unable to prove any damage to the consumer...because there were no damages to the consumer.

"The agreement presented to the court represented a mutual decision among all of the defendants. We believe it's a fair settlement for all parties, giving consumers coupons as a form of discount for milk purchases, which are available to anyone who had been a bona fide Arizona resident between 1969 and early 1978—something for everybody. The dairies and retail chains get relief from expensive court appearances. Shamrock's portion of the settlement, for instance, is less than our estimate of the costs of attorneys' fees to continue to a complete victory....The agreement states: 'No part of the amount paid by the settling defendants is paid as a penalty, fine, punitive damages, or other form of assessment for any offense.' " [13]

"Rigorous competition, acknowledged to be the fallout from the antitrust cases, supplied a great environment for Shamrock," wrote David L. White, one of the Shamrock attorneys assigned to the case. "In an industry where success was subsequently based strictly on quality and efficiencies, Shamrock has done very, very well. Shamrock did not need or want an industry that protected any company from competition. It has thrived when just the opposite is true. Thus, to the extent the antitrust litigation might have provided for an atmosphere of tough competition on the merits, Shamrock is thankful." [14]

Norman McClelland

In looking back to learn from the past, I see Shamrock's transition from a very small dairy company playing the role of follower or tag-along in an industry of giant dairy companies to today when we are leading the market in our dairy division and both food divisions. The habits we had as a small company with a one-price system to all customers were not possible as our customer mix changed from mom-and-pop grocery stores to giant grocery and food-service customers. We learned from the antitrust violations as a small dairy company and today strictly enforce a code of conduct at Shamrock, not only to comply with the law but to deal with no competitors at any level and to continue to focus on a policy of dealing only with customers and making every effort to serve our customers' needs. [15]

Raw milk is stored in giant silos at the Phoenix plant,
the tallest has a 60,000 gallon capacity.

Denver food distribution warehouses and offices.

The Arizona Foods Division offices and warehouse in Phoenix, 1995.

An artist's rendering of mid-1990s expansion of the Arizona Foods Division necessitated by installation of a sophisticated automated storage and retrieval system.

Frances McClelland, daughter of Shamrock's founders and
the longtime secretary-treasurer on the Board of Directors.

Norman McClelland, Shamrock's president since 1954, became its chairman in 1992.

Kent McClelland, president of Shamrock Foods Company since 1992.

*Shamrock Foods Company's Board of Directors, 1996, left to right: David Hall,
senior vice president; Oliver Stallings, assistant secretary; Norman McClelland, chairman;
Kent McClelland, president; Frances McClelland, secretary-treasurer.*

Shamrock Foods Company management group, 1993

Arizona Foods Division early morning food delivery to the Wigwam Resort.
Left to right: Cecil Ravenswood, general manager of the Wigwam, executive chef John Hill, and
Joe Heffey, Shamrock driver.

Shamrock refrigerated air-conditioned tractor-trailers crisscross
vast areas of Southwestern desert to deliver orders.

An Arizona family shopping for milk products.

Morgan Ghormley, who named Shamrock Farms' famous ice cream cow, Roxie.

Chapter Thirteen

Mega-Warehousing

*T*en years after entering the Colorado food-service arena, Shamrock acknowledged that the volume of business was fast outgrowing its facilities. By 1980,
when sales and inventory requirements were beginning to outstrip warehouse
capacity, it was clear that something major had to be done. In March 1981, a
twenty-three-and-a-half-acre parcel in Commerce City near the old Denver
airport was acquired, and the Barrett Company was hired to do a complete
study of the division's products and product flow and, ultimately, to design
a warehouse facility that would hold the wide variety of product lines the
company distributed. The design had to allow for the future expansion of all
departments and to incorporate a computerized storage-and-retrieval system to
control floating inventories.

The building site was originally a pig farm, complete with barn and farm-
house. Not only did the old structures have to be razed before new construction could begin but tons of pig manure also had to be removed. Future lawn
growth was compromised somewhat by residual manure elements in the soil.

When the warehouse floor plan was completed, a decision was made to
commission an engineering firm, rather than a team of architects, to design the
building. The chosen firm was A. V. Schwan & Associates of Phoenix, and engineer-architect Tony Schwan was assisted by Chuck Andrews, who acted as

building overseer for Shamrock. Fritz Covillo became responsible for much of the interior design, including the offices, showroom, and entrance area.

Excavation of the new building began in June 1982, and the building itself was completed the following April, by which time United Food Service had become Shamrock Foods Company of Colorado. Also at that time a tabletop equipment line was added, and the distribution rights to Continental Coffee were acquired, adding 500,000 pounds of coffee annually from that acquisition to Shamrock's already established beverage department. Thus by late spring 1983, Shamrock Foods of Colorado had become a truly full-line food-service and distributing company.

To celebrate the opening of the new warehouse, a gala VIP dinner party and dedication were held in May. Local officials, executives from Shamrock in Arizona and others instrumental in creating the new facility were invited to tour the building and view the company's new equipment and expanded product lines. In June, Shamrock hosted a grand opening food show that enabled customers and suppliers alike to see the product and tour the new facility.

What they saw was cutting-edge design contained in a two-and-a-half-story 200,000-square-foot complex that included office space plus a circular tabletop and restaurant equipment showroom displaying such disparate items as china, flatware, bud vases, coolers, gas ranges, and meat slicers. But it was the warehouse facility itself that was more than just a real estate landmark for Shamrock; it had been designed not only "to maintain the highest quality of product but also to enable employees to handle stocking, receiving and loading with utmost speed, accuracy and safety," according to David Timmons, writing in the *Shamrock News*.[1]

DAVID "DAVE" TIMMONS
Former Shamrock employee in Colorado

The refrigerated portion of the warehouse includes six computer-controlled fruit-ripening rooms, a unique low ceiling in the loading area to help maintain proper temperatures, loading docks cooled to sixty degrees, wet and moderate humidity refrigerated-produce rooms, and one of Colorado's largest working deep freezers.

To further increase quality control and handling efficiency of fresh and frozen foods, all meat, fish, poultry, and produce buyers have offices located in the dock area of the warehouse. Buyers can, therefore, immediately inspect products upon delivery rather than several hours later when valuable time would be wasted if the products were unacceptable and had to be returned to suppliers.

The dry-foods area is extremely well organized and is not only heated to proper storing temperatures when necessary but is also fully air-conditioned. Floors are specially hardened to withstand the constant onslaught by the forklifts. An in-house forklift maintenance station is available for immediate repairs on machinery.

Two techniques are used to guarantee rapid turnover of product and excellent retrieval efficiency in the warehouse. P.I.R. (planned item retrieval) is an innovative computerized selection system which allows a product to be placed where there is an opening on the shelf. A computer records the location and the date the product is received so products can be removed quickly and in chronological order. Shamrock of Colorado spared nothing when it came to equipping and laying out the warehouse, and we tried to make sure the rest of the building conveyed our fast becoming recognized "leader of the pack" image as well.[2]

To sustain its leadership role, the Commerce City operation had to continue to expand and did so until it, too, began to outgrow its facilities. In May 1989, ground was broken for a $6.5 million addition that would bring total warehouse space to 270,000 square feet. There were five new offices and an addition of 45,000 square feet to the existing 75,000 square feet of dry storage plus a bonus of 15,000 square feet of dry dock space. Perhaps the most interesting statistics, as reported by Jan Wascher and Larry Noble in the *Shamrock News*, involved design of the new freezer.

JAN WASCHER AND LARRY NOBLE
Former Colorado operations employees

The new freezer is 45,000 square feet, plus 15,000 square feet of thirty-five-degree dock. Refrigeration units for the freezer are located on the roof of the building, for easier maintenance. The bottom layer is a rock-aggregate temperature barrier which keeps the ground below the freezer from freezing, expanding, and buckling the finished floor. The next layer is a five-inch-thick concrete sub-floor to cap the rock. Then a five-inch layer of high-density foam insulation is added as an additional temperature barrier. Finally, a six-inch layer of super-flat, hardened concrete finish floor is added. This allows our warehouse equipment to operate safely and smoothly all the way up to our clear storage height of forty-five feet.[3]

Larry Noble also reported that, because storage needs had become so acute by the time the addition was under construction, Shamrock "actually reopened the old building, which is about three and a half miles from the new one, and we were operating out of two warehouses from June '89 through February '90."[4]

Larry had joined the company as a driver in 1979, and little more than a year later, according to Dave Hall, "the drivers voted—and elected him a supervisor, the youngest one in the company."[5] From delivery supervisor he became, first, transportation manager, warehouse manager, and then in 1991, at age thirty-four, operations manager for the Colorado Foods Division. In this capacity he had the responsibility of overseeing the daily flow of product in and out of the warehouse and also keeping a sharp eye on future needs. Late in 1994, he was looking closely at the old 25,000-square-foot freezer, which had been shut down in 1990 when the new facility was operational, then reopened little more than a year later and leased to American Storage Company. "They have been very good tenants," he reported, "but we're about at the point that we'll be asking them to leave because we need the space for future refrigerated products."[6]

The warehouse has ripening rooms for tomatoes, bananas, and avocados and rooms at various temperatures for meat, fish, fresh produce, ice cream, and other frozen products and, of course, for dairy items, which are trucked from Phoenix six times a week. Larry pointed out that one big difference between the Colorado and Arizona food-service operations is that traditionally there was a greater emphasis on produce in Colorado because of the company's long history in produce through the Mozer and Covillo family businesses.

Larry confirmed the fact that the Colorado division was equipped to provide almost total service to a customer. "We can do the kitchen design, the steam tables, the walk-ins, the cleanups—every mop, bucket, broom, chemical and all the other janitorial supplies — in short, provide everything except alcoholic beverages and the building itself," he noted.[7]

Nearly everything was computerized by the mid-'90s in a mega-warehouse stocked with 14,000 line items. Labels and customer invoices printed out by computers directed forklift operators to fill complete orders and also told them where to go to find each item. All the improvements and systems refinements that had been made to date, and planned for the future, were designed to make the receiving, storage, and retrieval processes more efficient, less labor intensive and generally faster. "We're always looking to shrink the time frame," said Larry. "If you shorten the time from when you get an item till it's on its way to the customer, you can make room for more products that can be processed for the same dollars. Right now we have a $13 million inventory in just one building."[8] And that building was designed with the potential to house a totally automated retrieval system. "It was a unique approach in the way we designed it," Larry observed, "and the Phoenix setup is going to be identical because we designed it together."[9]

When Kent Mullison joined the Colorado operation as controller late in 1983, after eight years with the Coopers and Lybrand accounting firm, he recalled becoming aware of the turmoil associated with moving to the new warehouse. "It was a fairly large move," he remembered, "and there was a change in our computer system at the same time. So we had just come through a period where we couldn't track our inventories, the trucks were late every day, we didn't know what was going on—except that it was causing havoc with our customers. We had gone through the worst of it by the time I came aboard in November, but there was still quite a bit of chaos." [10]

KENT MULLISON
Vice President and General Manager of the Colorado Division

In August of that year there had been a large write-off, which was devastating to everyone. Everyone had been excited about the new building, then a few months later all the errors got written off. It was a terrible month; people were rebounding from that. The warehouse crew had been able to adjust to the new facility fairly quickly, but people working in the office felt the difference for some time.

Although I'd never worked in the old building, one of the comments I heard over and over was that everyone had been much closer there. It had been, basically, one big room where everyone sat: all the salespeople and a lot of the clerical people. Everyone communicated all the time, then they got into this nice new building and everything was compartmentalized—sales was in one place, purchasing in another, accounting in another—so communication dropped off. That was a concern for quite a while; people still talk about it. [11]

Kent became general manager of the division in October 1991 and continued to work closely with Kent McClelland until McClelland moved back to

Phoenix a year or so later. (Tom Haberkorn, who had joined the company in 1989, succeeded Kent Mullison as controller.) Mullison felt his biggest challenge, in moving the division forward, was to continue to meld each of the many acquisitions into one and, without compromising any of the components, to establish a distinctly Shamrock culture. After all, he said a few years later, each company had contributed its own distinctive culture, the largest one, of course, being United Food Service.

KENT MULLISON

What's made me happiest was when the Colorado division finally started to mature and come into its own, when we felt we were a full-fledged part of the corporation. When I first got here, people continually asked me, "Aren't you from Phoenix?" The assumption was that you had to have come from Arizona. You can't be from Colorado, because that's not the way it works.

Over the years we've built a good team of managers and associates that trust each other and the corporation perhaps more than in the past. Although we've always worked together very well, there has been some scar tissue from the many acquisitions. I think it took about eleven years for people to stop saying "I'm a United person" or "I'm a Mile Hi person" and begin saying they were Shamrock people.[12]

As late as the mid-'90s the Colorado division was still a mix—of new employees and those who had worked for companies that had been absorbed into the division. According to Kent Mullison, most of the people in the receiving crew had been with the company a long time, "but the night crew, the shipping crew, was mainly new people."[13]

Kent Mullison

Our goal is to be able to receive and ship simultaneously, and to be receiving and shipping twenty-four hours a day. We hope to reach the point where a customer calls in an order and within two hours a truck is rolling toward his location, whether he's in Santa Fe or Commerce City.

We reach about a 450-mile radius. We go as far south as Albuquerque and as far north as Casper, Wyoming. We go to North Platt, Nebraska, and then to the western border of Colorado. Now we also go into a corner of Utah. The Arizona division handles southern New Mexico, we handle the north, and we sort of come together right about Albuquerque but really don't overlap. We have enough competition without competing with each other.[14]

Larry Noble happily anticipated a time, perhaps by the year 2000, when the Colorado warehouse would be fully mechanized.

Larry Noble

Here's how an automated storage-and-retrieval system would work: A pallet is received much the same way we've always done it, and a label with a bar code is put on that pallet. The fork operator scans it with a hand-held R.F. (radio-frequency) device that is actually receiving the product. The R.F. not only records the arrival of the product but actually updates the inventory in the computer a pallet at a time. Next, the receiver picks up the pallet, sets it on a conveyor belt that takes it to a crane. The crane, unmanned, picks up the pallet and puts it away.

During the selection process, if a slot becomes empty, then a crane goes, picks up the overstock, and puts it into that location.

In the selection phase, there are still individuals walking down the aisles with stickers. They peel each sticker off, put it on a box, pick up the box, and place it on the conveyor belt, which takes each box all the way into a waiting truck. An individual in the truck will pick up the box and stack it.

What we've eliminated is driving around in the tuggers and carts, covering the entire building during the selecting process. We've also eliminated the man on the forklift restocking the slots at night, but we haven't eliminated the manual element entirely. There is still somebody inside the truck accepting the boxes and stacking them, and there is still somebody at the other end of the conveyor picking them up and putting them on the conveyor.

Our manpower needs may not change very much as new systems are introduced, though our costs will probably rise. In a mechanized system such as we're developing, when you start running ten- or fifteen-mile conveyor belts through this building, a lot of maintenance will be required to keep it running—mechanics and supervisors in addition to the clerical component. But, overall, I think we can look to at least a fifty percent improvement in productivity.[15]

He also looked to continued growth in market share within the region served by the division and by the year 2000 perhaps another expansion of the warehouse.

LARRY NOBLE

This time, we would probably add on to the building behind the addition—there's room to do that—and we would probably construct the mechanization there first, which would allow us to move some of the products in there while we convert the front part of the warehouse. It's tough to keep doing business while converting to a new system warehouse. In Phoenix, they will add sections to the building totally, and then move into them. In Commerce City, I would see us probably adding to the rear of the building, having it set up and then adding a front porch, which would take a little bit longer.

This wouldn't halt our productivity growth, but it would slow us down at times. It would take a year to put in conveyor belts, for example. In Phoenix, from the time they say OK, when they start building and actually engineering the mechanized warehouse, they're talking about two years.

Another thing that's a real concern for me, from an operating point of view, is the effectiveness of backup systems. If something happens and the system goes down and the conveyors aren't moving, you cannot conventionally "pick" a mechanized warehouse—not with stuff that's forty feet off the ground. You need backup computer systems, backup power generator systems, and good mechanics, so that if something goes down, you can get it up and running again.

With the necessary racking, the cranes and the computer systems required to run them, not to mention the building itself, building a fully mechanized warehouse is a multimillion-dollar investment. I'm glad Phoenix is going to do it first.[16]

Actually, the Phoenix Dairy had made its first gesture toward total mechanization back in the sixties with casers and stackers, equipment that would lift filled bottles off of the production line, place the bottles in cases moving along a conveyor belt, and, finally, stack the cases one atop another. Three decades later, in the spring of 1994, Kent McClelland pointed out that the two L-shaped additions being engineered then would add 75,000 square feet to the Arizona food-service warehouse in Phoenix. When completed, each would stand ninety feet tall and be serviced with automated cranes plus an automated storage-and-retrieval system. There would be no structural columns in either L; the racks themselves would become the supporting bones around which the skin of the structure would be stretched.

"This is the first phase of our planned expansion," Kent explained. "Everything that's built here is erected with the future in mind and an emphasis on efficiency, cost effectiveness, and finding the right labor for the right activity."[17] As in Colorado, Tony Schwan, the engineer-architect for Shamrock building projects for over twenty-five years, lent his capable hand to the process.

Kent McClelland said that $40 million had been assigned to the expansion program that would triple the capacity of the Phoenix food facility over a ten-year period. "It has already started," said Bob Gray in 1993. "We redid the roof of our warehouse on Virginia Avenue. Instead of just putting on a normal one-inch-thick roof, we put in four inches of foam insulation plus three coatings on top of that, so now we have the outer envelope for our cooler of the future. The cooler will be part of our first phase, and then we'll build a new freezer and dry storage facility outside the existing building."[18]

BOB GRAY

In our next phase, we'll be building a long receiving dock that, by the end of '96, should be receiving all our frozen, refrigerated, and dry products. Then, simultaneously, we'll be building another long receiving dock where the trucks will back in and where our automated conveyor system will feed those trucks. It's an amazing process to see, as it's all based on a bar-coded label, laser scanning, and automatic computer-driven sorters. The conveyor extends all the way into the truck; it has a light on it and the driver will have a little document map showing where to load everything at the time he's throwing his cases off. Right now, one person averages about 190 cases an hour; with this system he should be able to handle 400 cases because of the cut in travel time. Everything will be very condensed.[19]

Pickers will continue to play a significant role in the future warehouse, but they will operate on foot instead of on tuggers and carts, and they will feed conveyor belts running down the middle of each aisle.

BOB GRAY

The picker will simply walk beside this moving belt, pick a case off the shelf, put a label on it, and put it on the belt. The belt will take it past a sorter, a laser scanner such as you would find at a supermarket checkout, which will scan that label and send it— through a series of converters—to the conveyor belt that will make sure it ends up in the back of the appropriate truck.

Another part of the new automated system consists of computer-operated trains like forklifts designed to run up and down a track unmanned. You take a pallet off the receiving dock and put it on an inbound station. What's on the pallet has bar-coded labels on it. The system "reads" the pallet and asks, in effect, "Is it square? Is it the right height?" and runs it on farther. The train will automatically pick up the pallet and, "knowing" the inventory, will decide, "Do I need it in the pick? Do I need it in the reserve?" After it determines where to place the pallet, it also says, "While I'm back there I'm going to move three more pallets in the reserve to pick, because I know I'm going to need them." Every decision will be made by computer.[20]

Bob noted that in the event of an occasional mispick, a laser scanner will tell the picker that the wrong item has been selected. A correction can be made well before an item reaches the truck. The ultimate goal is not only speed and efficiency in receiving, storing, and shipping products but also in total customer satisfaction and achieving the perfect order.

According to Larry Yancy, general manager of the Arizona Foods Division, the perfect order "has no out-of-stock, no errors, and is delivered within the time window the customer has designated. In other words, no credit memos would be written against it, no returns would take place or anything else that would count it as less than a perfect order."[21] This thrust toward total customer satisfaction was a mandate of Larry's from the time he took over the division in 1992 when Dave Hall retired. Larry had grown up in the food-service business. His father had been the warehouse superintendent of a Phoenix-based company called Smart & Final Iris Company, and Larry himself had been a partner in his own business until it was acquired by Kraft Foods, then five years later he became part of the Shamrock family. As general manager, one of his primary concerns was to sustain and increase the company's growth curve. Total customer satisfaction was one approach he took.

In 1992 there were 51 percent perfect orders; two years later the average had jumped more than 20 points. "We think that 87 to 90 percent is achievable without having to adjust our inventory to a ridiculous level," he said.[22] Just making people aware of errors and of the long-term impact on customer relations was the first step in correcting them. Integrating new automatic equipment compounded the challenge, but total customer satisfaction and a thrust toward the "perfect order" became ongoing objectives: not easily reached but always in sight. Larry had a more immediate challenge to confront at the time he came aboard. "The first project Dave Hall wanted me to tackle was to get a sales jump started."[23]

LARRY F. YANCY
Vice President and General Manager of Arizona Foods Division

I recall that one of the first things I did was meet with the sales staff and find out what their perceptions were, what in their eyes was going on with the customers, and why we were not growing more. One of the things we discovered in our core markets, the

Phoenix and Tucson metropolitan areas, was that though we had grown over the years, we had not really added equipment or people to service these markets. And since these markets were growing more rapidly than others, it was clear that we were not keeping up with these markets in terms of providing appropriate support.

That was the number-one issue. Number two was the fact that our purchasing department was not very flexible in meeting the needs of either customers or salespeople. It had become somewhat rigid in terms of what it was prepared to stock, perhaps losing sight of our customers' needs. So our thrust was to try to identify areas in need of strengthening and at the same time to pinpoint markets in which we could grow if we could successfully recruit talented salespeople, which we did. We also started listening to our customers a little bit more, responding with improved service, and striving to get the departments to work together more closely for customer satisfaction.[24]

A particular goal of Larry's was to encourage his sales staff to look carefully at the margins and at order sizes—in order to penetrate their accounts more effectively with more product or product categories than, historically, they had been buying. "In other words," Larry explained, "if they're ordering dairy products, try to get their produce business. If you get dairy and produce, try to get their nonfood business, their paper goods, their carryout supplies. Our marketing strategy is to be a broad-line distributor."[25]

LARRY YANCY

We already knew where the customers were, and we knew how our customers paid their bills. What we needed to do was try to sell them more cases for more dollars each time we go there—and not worry so much about trying to get ten new customers as penetrating the accounts we already have. Not only does that give you a greater dollar margin, it also decreases your expenses.

I was concerned that we were putting too much emphasis at times on center-of-the-plate items—the prime rib, the chicken breast, the fresh fish—and not enough emphasis on some of the more profitable categories. It's fine to sell the chicken and beef, but let's also sell our customers the pots and pans, paper goods, cleaning chemicals, and, naturally, dairy products—and drive those order sizes up to become more profitable in nature. We should be trying to penetrate our accounts with anything we manufacture: shortening and oil, for example.

Once we felt we were well on our way to selling to our customers in greater depth, we could focus on expanding that customer base and looking to other geographical markets. Our strategy involving the mega-warehouse concept dictates that we open up other geographical markets to support the thrust of our automation and mechanization. New geographical markets mean increased costs, which we don't want to incur unless there is good reason to do so—such as having saturated the existing market and needing room to grow. The key is, you want to really have a lot of volume going through a system like this.

We're trying to plan for the year 2005, based on a current projection of ten-percent pace growth per year. We may or may not be able to handle such growth out of this facility. At some point we may have to develop another warehouse and take some of the volume out of here—perhaps build a facility in southern California or buy one and move that volume there. From our current volume, in the neighborhood of $350 million a year, with the growth we're planning, we could reach $750 million by the target year.[26]

As with the two food divisions, versatility has been the hallmark of the dairy division and, from the beginning, perhaps the core secret of its phenomenal growth. "There are some plants as large as we are, west of the Mississippi, but they don't do cottage cheese, sour cream, buttermilk, juices, and ice cream mixes as we do," said operations chief Bob Gromko. "We are not the largest or most complicated milk plant in the country, but we're certainly one of the largest plants that make all of the products we do."[27]

Much of the dairy division's expansion can be credited to the continual upgrading that has taken place since the plant was completed in 1956. New storage tanks and freezers have replaced old ones, new conveyor systems have helped accelerate milk processing, new vats for sour cream and buttermilk have been installed, new automated systems have been introduced—all with the single goal of moving product through the processing plant faster, shortening the time span from the moment raw milk arrives until it leaves on trucks, in containers, cartons, and packages. "Remember," Bob added, "the process is pretty simple, but it's the key to making milk fit to drink: It must be heated to 161½ degrees for sixteen seconds."[28]

By the early nineties the process had been refined to such an extent that seven thousand gallons an hour could pass through the entire heating, cleaning, skimming, mixing, and homogenizing process. "That means two minutes for a drop of milk to make it through the system," said Bob.[29] He looked ahead to a time, perhaps after the turn of the century, when milk could be treated at higher temperatures—in effect, sterilized—so that it would no longer be a perishable product, thus wouldn't require refrigeration.

BOB GROMKO

I argue with myself as much as anyone else, but if we haul a forty-foot trailer load of milk to a supermarket every day, what in the world is the advantage of being able to take in thirty days' worth of milk? What would we do? Take in thirty trailer loads of milk one day and not take any for a month? It makes no sense. No retailer could store thirty days' worth of milk. So the impetus to have a shelf-stable product is not necessarily there.[30]

Still, the need for more and more storage continued to mount. "You need storage so that you can have all of the products available for all the trucks all the time," Bob pointed out. "We cannot store a whole day's production; we have to manufacture and load out at the same time, which we do."[31]

A key moment, central to the concerted growth statewide of Shamrock's dairy business, occurred in the late eighties when it was decided that the Tucson plant would merge its volume with the Phoenix operation. Left behind would be only a sales force and a small clerical team to serve southern Arizona directly.

BOB GROMKO

Traditionally, they did ice cream mixes, purified water, and the juices in Tucson. In Phoenix we did the milk, cottage cheese, sour cream, buttermilk, and chocolate milk. We're no longer in the water business, but all of the other functions are being done in the Phoenix plant. We had to get this plant in condition to run the soft ice cream mixes, the orange juice, and other juices. Ice cream mixes are demanding; they require a process that is totally different from the other milks. The juices, too, require a totally different process. Making the transition was very complex because we had to sustain the business we had while building to capacity to handle the new systems we were taking on.

We did it in two phases. We moved the fresh milk portion of the Tucson plant into Phoenix in April of 1989. We completed the transition of the mixes and the juices two months later. Some of the equipment was moved up and we were able to use it—the blow-mold machine, for example, plus some refrigeration equipment.

Other equipment that did not make sense to move was sold until the plant was completely empty.[32]

As luck and history would have it, the Tucson operation did continue to function as part of the distribution network. Despite Shamrock's determination to deal with customers in Tucson exactly the way customers in Phoenix were treated, the reality was that the Tucson stores were nearly two hours away.

BOB GROMKO

Our philosophy was not to store anything in Tucson, to simply load our trucks in Phoenix, go to the stores—wherever they were— and deliver the product. Practically speaking, that approach works fine for the larger stores, but for the smaller stores it's not feasible to pull up in a forty- or forty-five-foot trailer and take off three cases of milk, then go on to the next store and do the same thing. So we have some smaller routes running in Tucson. And our theory is that we will preload those smaller routes on a big truck, go to Tucson, take them off of large truck A, reload it on smaller truck B, and deliver the product without its ever going into storage.

It was a great theory, as theories go; however, there were some timing problems and logistical kinks that compelled us to make use of a small cooler in Tucson. Of course, wherever possible we don't handle the product at all after it's loaded here in Phoenix; we move and deliver it on the same truck. But where that is not possible, we try to move it directly from truck A to truck B. And if *that* is not possible, we let it come to rest in the Tucson facility. Probably there will always be a facility in Tucson to serve an operation that's 120 miles away.

As a company, we have always planned and made projections as to what we thought would happen with our growth. The company

makes projections in dollar sales numbers, but in the dairy division
we look at it in gallons, and we have created five-year plans that
have always seemed outlandish and unbelievable, but we've had to
live with them. To my knowledge, we have exceeded every projection we ever made, especially the ones we considered impossible.
We still look at numbers that we're not sure we'll ever attain, but
based on past history we probably will. When it opened, the
Phoenix dairy plant ran 10,000 gallons of milk a day, then went to
80,000 gallons, and now it's 180,000 gallons a day. Is it possible that
someday we could have a 300,000-gallon-a-day milk plant or a
400,000-gallon-a-day plant? That's one of the questions I personally struggle with: Just how large can a plant get? And, of course,
there is no answer to that. Yet.[33]

Growth was one of the many topics under analysis and discussion when
Norman, Frances, and Kent McClelland convened a meeting of Shamrock general managers and senior-level corporate people in May 1993. According to
Kent, the purpose of the meeting was "to take us through a look at the future
and try to see what our strengths and weaknesses were and how we could best
use our strengths and shore up our weaknesses in order to stay around for the
next seventy or a hundred years."[34]

The name the group assigned itself was Vision 2000, and the conclusions it
drew from discussions that took place became a road map for the company to
follow on its way to the millennium.

KENT MCCLELLAND

One of the conclusions we drew was that our warehouses had
become so complex that it was best to have just a few of them. We
decided that we would build big ones and service large regions
out of them and, for reasons of efficiency and scale economy, place

fairly heavy emphasis on technology. That was a departure from what we had done before, because earlier we had experimented with smaller facilities and decided it was not practical to expand market share or our distribution network through satellite warehouses.

Another conclusion we reached was that we did want to continue to grow faster than the market is growing in all of the categories we sell. We wanted to do that and thought we could best do it through these mega-warehouses, whose care and feeding is demanding. You've got to have a lot of volume to support them. We would consider building in any market where we have enough volume to be able to justify and sustain a mega-warehouse—something like what we're in now or even larger. Where mega-warehouses are concerned, as long as you've got a lot of volume going through them, their costs are justifiable. Capital costs are pretty high, but the labor savings are great.[35]

The strategy Shamrock traditionally followed has been bolstered by growth in the marketplace. "But that's not the whole story by any stretch," Michael Krueger insisted. "The key to it has been Norman's own dedication to growing our market share—so that even if the economy was flat or declining, we would still continue to gain a competitive advantage. As it happened, while we were growing market share, we were also experiencing a strong economy, so our growth became almost explosive."[36]

Mike Krueger joined the Arizona Foods Division in 1978, quickly rising from salesman to sales supervisor. He became the company's first national accounts manager, then relocated to Colorado to become general sales manager in that operation. Within a year of returning to the dairy division in Phoenix in 1993, Derrell Fairfield retired and Mike succeeded him as general manager of the dairy division, working closely with Richard Brooks, the division's longtime vice president of sales.

Mega-Warehousing

Michael "Mike" Krueger
Vice President and General Manager of the Dairy Division

Growth wasn't explosive for any of our competitors, yet they were sitting here in the same vibrant marketplace and weren't doing anything about it—because while the market was experiencing six to eight percent a year growth, they may have been growing four to six percent. So their growth rate was slower than the market as a whole while we were growing continually at a rate of fifteen to twenty percent per year. We were the ones expanding our product lines; we were the ones adding to our warehouse facility.

I think Norman was the single individual in the entire marketplace who had that kind of aggressive commitment to growing the business. He was willing to take some risks and to support the kinds of things that we were able to do that no one else did. I think he was a real visionary—at times maybe a little bit like a riverboat gambler—and he was absolutely committed to that course.

I believe that Kent McClelland has that same level of commitment to continue building the business. I see him as an advocate of continuing to grow market share, and I believe that through such growth comes competitive advantages and economies of scale that will allow us to further grow our market share and differentiate from our competition in what will become a perpetuating cycle.

I also see Kent as the champion of the quality movement. And what that will empower us to do is tap into the resources of all the people at Shamrock through a team approach to running the business. This will enable us—as we continue to grow very large as a company—to act very small in terms of staying close to our customers, being able to respond quickly and efficiently to their needs. I think that's the prime challenge for any company as it increases in size: to figure out how to keep the bureaucracy from strangling itself.

And I believe preventing that will add to our ability to continue growing and to grow successfully as we go forward.[37]

Chapter Fourteen

The Team Concept

*T*he idea was new in the food-service business, but not in the world of commerce. Kent McClelland began pondering its possible impact on Shamrock when he went to Colorado in the eighties. During an eighteen-month period after he became president of that division, he and other Shamrock executives called on a number of companies around the country, among them Xerox and Federal Express, to see how they were organized and structured. The idea was to find model companies to look to and learn from.

According to Kent, the most successful and most forward-thinking corporations had been able to drive out waste, eliminate redundancy, and compress layers of management by establishing team-based organizations within their corporate structures. For Shamrock, Kent reasoned, this might be a way to provide extraordinary customer service, which would spur growth and make the company even more competitive in the markets it served.

Team management had the potential to transform more and more employees from minor players to major participants, people with greater access to and responsibility for their customers. It was a concept that rang true for Shamrock, which had been established according to Mr. Mac's original notion of treating employees like family and customers like friends. The concept implied a kind of intimacy no longer possible in an expanding company built on many layers of management. "As we got bigger, it got harder," said Kent.[1]

Kent McClelland

The more people who are directly involved in serving the customers, the better chance you have of serving those customers well,
meeting their needs, and keeping them long term. And you can be
more profitable doing all that because you become more capable of
meeting their requirements at a lower cost, thus at a fair price,
which is another part of our philosphy.

A small company has a certain advantage, because everybody is
involved in just about everything. As a company grows larger, as we
have done, it becomes fragmented. You have manufacturing here,
sales there, then shipping and transportation, but none of it is tied
together primarily to meet customer requirements. Everyone gets
locked in to little compartments, and the focus starts shifting from
the customer, which is where it started, to a manager or a level of
managers, which is not where it belongs. The focus should be shifted back to the customers, as they are the final arbiters of our success
as a business. If we can focus on our customers, and get more and
more people involved in the process of meeting customer requirements more efficiently and effectively than the competition, then we
can keep our customers a long time and become more successful in
furthering our growth.[2]

Larry Yancy echoed Kent's feelings, recalling that when he joined the
Institutional Foods Division he found it highly segmented.

Larry Yancy

Some shoring up was needed. Our division wasn't growing
as rapidly as it once had been, and we were getting stiff competition
in the area of customer service, which is what had built the business

over the years. What I was hearing throughout the division was, "I'm in transportation...or purchasing...or distribution," and there was not as much involvement in customer problems or issues as there should be. Everyone seemed part of some segregated entity, and the larger the division had become, the bigger each of those functional departments was getting.

Also, it had become harder than ever to maintain the close-knit family atmosphere that had always been Shamrock's strength. I felt it was necessary to try to knock down some of those walls, so to speak, and get people to start communicating and working together—and to realize that we needed to focus more on the customer rather than on our individual job descriptions or the mandates of each of our departments.[3]

The companies to which Kent and other Shamrock executives made formal visits had each been recipients of the Baldridge National Quality Award, named after a former secretary of the interior. The Baldridge Award is presented to world-class companies in recognition of the superlative way they manage themselves. Along with the award, the companies are given the requirement of sharing insights into what has made them successful through seminars organized for representatives of other interested companies, even competitors.

Kent recalled attending a two-day event staged by Xerox. The first session was a general introduction to their business and the way their company was structured. The second session was subdivided according to specific interests: human resources or production, for example. Each company program offered food for thought, in a sense providing different pieces of a puzzle that Kent and others would finally put together specifically for Shamrock.

"Every business we saw was unique," Kent noted. "There was no one system we could adopt, nor could we take one idea from Xerox and one from Federal Express and say, 'This is our new management approach.' Instead, everything we observed became good fodder for helping us decide what the most appropriate structure for Shamrock should ultimately be."[4]

Visiting the Memphis, Tennessee, branch of Federal Express, for example, they were informed that when demands were greatest, upwards of eight thousand workers would be employed, though many on a part-time basis. In a traditionally structured firm of that size, there could be up to ten layers of management, but, astonishingly, the Memphis operation only had four. In their team-based environment, with very little supervision, Federal Express employees were able not only to organize themselves successfully but also to train new workers as well.

Two important discoveries were made during Shamrock's company visits. One was the significance of feedback, not only in measuring how well customers were being served but also in providing ways for managers to be evaluated by their peers. The other was confirmation of what Kent and his colleagues had already concluded— that the fewer layers of management, the better. More important than actual staff management was the need to understand what customers wanted, figure out how to do it at a profit and then devise ways and means to put walls around the customers so the competition would have a harder time reaching them.

Kent McClelland

There is such an enormous amount of potential input to be gleaned from the folks who are on the firing line every day: the folks who are driving the trucks, the folks who are making sales calls, the folks who are in the receivables and credit offices, the folks who are receiving the calls in customer service. But most of it isn't captured; it's lost—unless you have some sort of reward system, an incentive that makes it extremely important and valuable to listen to customers, understand their needs, and be creative enough to find a solution that meets these requirements and does so at a profit. The customers are the key to all of this; they are the ones who pay the bills.[5]

The idea of team management was placed high on the list of priority topics to discuss at the semiannual retreats held by each Shamrock division. The number-one question was how should the company organize itself. Second, but no less important, was how could personnel be redeployed to eliminate layers of management and focus the company on its own very specific needs. Through meeting after meeting, the shape of the teams began to be realized.

KENT MCCLELLAND

The first step was to reaffirm the fact that, in the distribution area, which is the biggest part of our business, there is an inbound function and an outbound function. We bring the product in, we get it ready for the customer, then we take the product out. There is a natural split. On the inbound side, we are turning specific functions into teams—like purchasing, accounts payable, inventory management, receiving, scheduling, and so forth, everything relating to products and services for our customers.

Traditionally, clerks in accounts payable were assigned vendors on an alphabetical basis—"you take A through M, or A to H." That makes sense only if your clerks have isolating tasks; then it's a good way to organize. But it has absolutely no bearing on what happens in purchasing or receiving. So what we're doing instead, on the inbound side, is putting together buyers and accounts-payable people and receiving clerks and receivers—people whose jobs are on the loading docks. And we are organizing them around product lines or around vendor bases or around temperature zones.

On the outbound side, the teams would include folks who select the orders, folks who load the trucks, folks who drive the trucks, and folks who take the orders to fill the trucks. We could just as easily organize them geographically as by segments, and by that I mean if we are focusing on the Mexican trade or the Italian pizza trade. Eventually we would hope that the boundary between inbound and outbound disappears and that we are organized simply from the vendor to the customer.[6]

The smooth merging of inbound and outbound services was not considered a pipe dream or a trial balloon. By the early nineties it was a reality in two food categories in the Colorado operation—fresh fish and the Asian segment—and each team was vendor-specific. After all, the unique needs of a Chinese, Korean, Japanese, or Vietnamese restaurant could not be met fully if purchasing and receiving were not linked to what was happening on the sales side. And knowledge of the market would be essential, across the board. "You have to buy right—in that market, for example, you have to buy shrimp and oil right," Kent pointed out.[7]

First to be fully restructured on a team basis was the Arizona Foods Division. Twenty-two teams were set up in 1993, five of them devoted to inbound, eleven to outbound, and the rest acting as support. "Support teams handle those functions that must be dealt with centrally," Larry Yancy insisted. "There is the centralized procurement of all trucks, for example, and the standardized reporting of industrial accidents. Otherwise the teams themselves are responsible for everything, for their own P and L, and also for their own hiring and discipline. Which means they are really empowered to deal with a lot of the functions that managers were responsible for before—a major shift, a cultural change for our company."[8]

Both Colorado and the dairy division took a more incremental approach to team management than Arizona Institutional Foods, which had completed some pilot programs successfully enough to convince Kent and Larry Yancy to take the plunge and make a sweeping reorganization. The most persuasive pilot study was called the Hyatt experiment; it was born of the hope that Shamrock could win the lucrative Hyatt Hotels business.

KENT MCCLELLAND

I suggested that we put a team of people together who would focus on Hyatt and really differentiate us from our competitors. Larry agreed that we should give it a try, so we put the selectors and the salespeople and the credit people together, and they visited all of the Hyatts to get answers to important questions: What are your requirements? What does your dock look like? What products do you want? Where do you want them stored? The Hyatt staff was accustomed to seeing drivers and salespersons, but this was the first time they were called on by selectors or floaters.

We agreed on a two-month rollout, and for two months we tracked the progress of the Hyatt team. The results were so staggering that even Hyatt couldn't believe it. Trucks arrived on time; there were no damaged goods; there were no mistakes—all of the pricing was correct. It was the smoothest possible transition, and usually the transition from one distributor to another can be very difficult.

During the designated time period we shipped something like 15,000 or 16,000 cases with no more than ten or twenty errors, all told. That, for us, was extraordinary. Such things never happen in our business. It's too complex. Too many things can go wrong. The success of that experiment convinced us that if organized right and orchestrated properly, the team concept would work for us in bringing in and servicing new customers.[9]

The concept of team management was the brainchild of two business consultants, W. Edward Deming and Joseph Juran, who presented it to General Motors back in 1945. GM could see no value in it, but Japanese businessmen seized on it as a way to rebuild their war-torn industries and ultimately profited hugely from it. Ironically, the United States' success in building a war machine quickly and efficiently, in the dark days following Pearl Harbor, resulted from deftly applied team-management techniques. But during the conversion back to manufacturing consumer goods, in the heady postwar years, it was business as usual for most of American industry.

Kent summed up the ramifications of the theory as simply letting customer requirements drive a business, and also as looking at the *process* instead of at the people, in order to achieve growth and improvement: "Teams work better than the pyramidal structure of a business organization because you don't have the bureaucracy, those entrenched layers of managment that are usually competing with one another."[10] Norman was an early adherent: "I like what Kent's doing along that line. It's a more thorough way of running a company and getting people involved at all levels of the organization."[11]

Ensuring the teams' ultimate effectiveness involves an enormous amount of training, getting people to understand the rhythm of the process and how to recognize the voice of the customer. An effective team doesn't need an inordinate amount of management, Kent pointed out. Essential to its success are good tools, good training and, as on the playing field, good quarterbacks and good coaches. "Some people are going to play the line, some people are going to play in the backfield—on both defense and offense," he said.[12]

For people whose training has led them into management, the team concept becomes a challenge to their adaptability, for instead of being in the position of directing staff, their job evolves into advising fellow team members, taking them aside to suggest new strategies, a realignment of duties or more effective ways to reach an objective. Coaches act as diplomats rather than dictators; most important, they must believe in the concept completely. "The team is setting the sails to get the best wind," said Kent, "but the coach is keeping the team on course."[13]

KENT MCCLELLAND

For a team member, the chance for job enrichment should be
huge. The cross-training opportunities, the ability to visit customers,
the chance to work with other team members and develop a different

set of skills—perhaps move around—would seem to be so much greater than before, when, for example, we might be hiring an accounts-receivable clerk and looking only for the skills related to that position. Now, an employee's clerical skills might be important to getting a job, but he or she would have to become familiar with all the disciplines, long term, to be of value to the team. And the team would be self-purifying in that regard. If a team member isn't performing, for whatever reason, it would be the job of the coach to say, "OK now, where are the gaps in your performance? How do we fill those gaps? What training do you need? What tools do you want that you don't have? How can we make you more effective?" It would be up to the coach to help that person contribute to the team.

Hopefully, we will reach the point where the selectors and loaders will go out with the rest of their team to visit top customers, looking through their warehouses to see what products they use and what they should be using in light of what we have to offer. When they come back to our warehouse at night and are at work, they will understand why they are choosing which product. They won't be simply loading cases but supplying products for their customers. It will be a similar first for the people who post the checks coming in from the customers to actually *see* who their customers are—and, more important, in terms of the larger, more demanding customers, to understand why they do what they do and come up with thoughts on how we can improve the process.[14]

Team size varies from twenty to forty members. It could be a little larger, but there will always be an effort to keep it under fifty to maintain a kind of family-size atmosphere and ensure that everyone feels included. Teams meet weekly at the beginning, then once or twice a month on a regular basis thereafter.

LARRY YANCY

A coach chairs the meetings. The primary responsibility of that coach is to be a facilitator, to get everybody involved—to interact, to discuss the issues. We ask a group of managers to select who they feel would be the best coach for each team according to its functions. Here, in Arizona Foods, we are fortunate in having management-level talent—men like Pete Burgoon, Jack Stipp, and Jack Waslefsky—playing key roles in this procedure. The coaches are trained to get the facts and then to analyze those facts before deciding how problems should be rectified.

Typically, a team will choose an assistant coach or a captain, if they wish. And that could be someone on the operational side to make sure those functions are flowing smoothly. So the team does have structure; it is responsible for keeping the process moving smoothly and is empowered to make decisions. The only qualifier is that if a team decides to make a change, it must communicate the fact of this change to other parallel teams. Let's say one outbound team wants to try picking orders in a different way. It would have to inform the other outbound teams that such an experiment was being planned and then, of course, communicate the results.[15]

Improved productivity, reduced waste, and better customer service are the target objectives of team management from the company point of view. What the employee stands to gain from team participation is not only a greater sense of involvement in customer relations but also financial participation in the success of the team. "What happens with team members in terms of being able to improve the quality element of their performance—no damage, no shorts, no mispulls—will have an impact on their compensation," Kent predicted. "For what the team does as a whole, every member can share in the rewards. If we do not tie the rewards to what the team is doing, the team concept will not work."[16] And what is the most significant indicator of the fact that it does work?

KENT McCLELLAND

An improvement in the level of service to our customers. We know where we are now. We know where we would like to be and we have a fair idea how we're going to get there. We think we can quantify fairly clearly what the difference between the new system and the old one is going to be in this particular arena.

Right now we measure our success in terms of perfect invoices, and our perfect-invoice level traditionally has been about seventy percent, companywide. That means thirty percent of the invoices that go out have something we will have to fix. It might be minor, but in the mind of the customer, a mistake is still a mistake and it hurts us. With the teams, I know we can eventually drive that percentage up to ninety or ninety-five, a huge difference and one that will give us a huge competitive advantage.[17]

Both Kent and Larry stressed the concept of sharing, from one team to another. Knowledge and information would be exchanged to keep competitors in sight and customer needs in sharp focus. Win-win would mark the relationship between teams, not win-lose.

LARRY YANCY

Team management involves change, and change is difficult, especially with a veteran work force that has been so successful. It's not as though we are being forced to change because we are destitute or ready to go out of business. But our new philosophy is that we must continuously improve the processes that serve our customers. And if we are not aligned to do that, we need to get aligned that way. And teams are one way of taking on responsibility for improving what we do. That is a big shift, I think.[18]

The significance of the change was pointed out by John Ceraulo, who joined the Arizona Foods Division in 1985. He worked for five years as major accounts manager and then became a regional sales manager, but the achievement he is proudest of is the creation of *Shamrock's Showcase,* a media piece he believed to be "as good as a trade magazine from a distributor's point of view."[19]

John described team management as "a concept that works toward narrowing the channel of communication, improving quality standards, reducing waste, and increasing profit margin. As such it is exciting, and it is dynamic!"[20]

But how does it affect the internal management structure of the company?

JOHN CERAULO
Team coach, Arizona Foods Division

It flattens the organization, which is no longer a silo pyramid. It changes from a vertically integrated management team to a horizontal management team. For example, internally the district sales manager is now a coach, the general sales manager is now a coach, the regional sales manager is now a coach. This does not in any way signify that these people are less than they would have been before; rather, they are more tied into quality and are also more accessible. Each is more identifiable as a member of a team and not part of a hierarchy. With communication barriers removed, there is more involvement, more straight-line level, flat team-based involvement— and a greater sense of participation.

The way I see it, the scope of my responsibilities has been enhanced through involvement with all the members of my team. I foresee having more time to function at my optimum skill level rather than being caught up in putting out fires or doing tasks twice because they weren't done properly the first time. For all of us, it means having more time to devote to improving skill levels, so that we can reach a point where we not only attain our goals but surpass them—beyond our own expectations.[21]

The coach is key to the success of the team, not because of professed managerial skills but because of possessing the ability to bring out the team's strength, the good ideas, the recommendations. Men like Al Aldrich, longtime sales manager in the Arizona Foods Division, can turn their experience and expertise into a laserlike teaching tool, influencing—without actually managing—the younger, equally talented but far less experienced team members. An effective coach empowers the players to be a process-based unit that analyzes problems in a no-fault environment—that is, without feeling intimidated.

JOHN CERAULO

Each player is important within his or her own function, just like the players in a ball club. No player can leave the team and have that team remain intact. And if, for example, the pitcher is having a bad day, pitching a poor game, the coach doesn't simply fire the pitcher when he goes out on the field. Instead, he finds out if and how he can help the pitcher, or maybe rests him on the bench for a few innings before putting him back in later. The objective is not to assign blame but to win the game.

The coach is not a boss; he's a supporter. The job takes patience; it also takes communication skills, conceptual skills and an enormous pledge of faith. The team's objective is to promote empowerment for process change recommendations.[22]

The recommendations are ongoing, and the goal, as always, is perfection. But, as John noted, it is only a goal. "Perfection is never possible; there is no such thing as achieving perfection.[23]

In the Colorado Foods Division, the concept of team management contributed at least partly to restoring the sense of community that had existed before the 1983 move to new quarters. As people became more acclimated to the building, they came to communicate more with each other and more willingly walked the extra steps they needed to take to meet with people in other departments. Kent Mullison attributed this successful interaction to the fact that the Colorado operation had never had the kind of internal boundaries that often exist in other companies.

KENT MULLISON

Here, people have elected to involve themselves pretty much in whatever they needed to in order to solve problems. It's traditional. Our managers have always communicated well and worked well together. No one has ever had qualms about talking to someone in another department about an issue and helping out, but one of the things we felt we really needed to focus on in Colorado was trust. Part of the reason for that is the culture here, with all the different people coming in from the different acquired companies and some of the scar tissue from the past.

Trust in this context could mean that I am looking at a control chart and may not be happy about the number of out-of-stocks for a particular day. But if I want to change that, I've got to change the entire process. I can't simply pin blame on the buyer, for it isn't the buyer's fault. It's the process, which is such that the buyer wasn't able to do the job the way we wanted, so we would have to examine the many different processes instead of pointing the finger at individuals.

Another element placed under scrutiny was *structure*. In all three divisions we took a look at our structure and decided it really wasn't impelling us forward in terms of helping our customers and raising our service level. With shared goals shaping our service to customers, accounts payable is no longer part of accounting; it's now part of the inbound team. And staff members not only share goals, they share work space and cross-train with the buyers so they are all working together as a team.

When you are structured by function and by department, you can sometimes be at odds. For example, if you're the transportation manager and you want to cut expenses and you're the general sales manager and your bonus is based on making deliveries, you're going to be locking horns. Where the sales manager would send a truck with one case on it, the transportation manager might say you've got to have a full truck. So they could conceivably be at odds with one another, We knew we needed to break through those artificial barriers between departments, and that's where the team concept came in.[24]

Results were immediately apparent in Colorado—not only in terms of productivity but also in terms of the quality of new personnel attracted to the company because of the direction it was taking. Similarly, according to Kent Mullison, a number of customer prospects materialized, asking to be briefed. "After receiving a presentation of what we were doing, they invited us out to visit them," he reported.[25] John Maier, appointed general sales manager of the Colorado Foods Division in 1991 after a career with Kraft, concurred that the new structure "is putting us far out in front of our competitors, and frankly, I cannot interview people fast enough who want to work here."[26]

JOHN MAEIR
Sales Manager, Colorado Foods Division

Work should be fun—I wish they called it something other than work. I think everyone here is having fun, and that's why we're going to be real tough competitors to deal with. What's fun is that there is active, dynamic participation by everyone at all levels of the organization. In a real sense, the company is the individual, for every individual in the organization has a vested interest in its success—coming up with the right decisions, correcting the processes, moving the company forward.

When I say that the company is the individual, I mean it's the night warehouse person being careful to make sure the right label is on the case; it's the driver making sure he is taking the right case to the customer; it's going every step along the way in our business to make sure the customer is satisfied. If everyone at every level within the organization is focused this way, how can anybody stop real progress? It's a terrific atmosphere.

I think the biggest challenge to me or anyone on the staff is learning to listen and learning to get out of the way a little bit. Your job title may tell you whom you're supposed to manage, but what I've learned is that when you manage the *process*, you don't have to manage the people.[27]

Robert Beake, who went to work as a route salesman upon joining the Colorado organization in 1979, could look back over the years at what he called a series of blue-sky plans that always received lip service and nods of agreement but had no long-lasting impact. The manager of national accounts since 1984, Bob could see that with each plan's diminution "we were losing the confidence of the work force. We had a great work force and a super company, but we weren't getting the results that we needed."[28]

230

ROBERT "BOB" BEAKE
National Accounts Manager, Colorado Foods Division

We finally adopted this team concept, the quality management concept, and it was Kent McClelland who really forced us to make it happen. He was relentless, and it paid off. Now we're all part of it. The entire organization is being trained—from the guys who sweep the warehouse floors to the drivers and sales staff. Everybody has become part of the decision-making process by being part of a team. And that's where we needed to get to make it work, so there is empowerment now at Shamrock.

I remember Kent's opening remarks at one of our January retreats. Anticipating the question of why we were moving in this direction, he wrote one word on the flip chart, "Survival." He agreed that we'd had a great year and could look forward to another one. That's fine, he said, but if we want to *survive*, we have to change. The great companies across the country are moving in this direction, and they will be the survivors. That kind of struck home with me; I knew I wanted to be part of the survival process.[29]

Kent McClelland's convictions were particularly evident when he stated, "The issue is not 'if it ain't broke, don't fix it'; in our case, it's 'let's make sure we fix it so it never will break.' "[30]

Chapter Fifteen

Four Businesses

*G*rowth. Expansion. Increased market share. Competitive value. Acquisitions. Consolidation. Mechanization. Computerization. Team management. Shamrock has undergone so many changes—so much progress—that the company might be virtually unrecognizable to anyone who was there at or near the start remembering what it was then compared to what it has become. Except for one thing: *its soul.* From the beginning, honesty and integrity have been its watchwords, and concern for the customer has always governed the way business has been done.

In a sense, then, the company hasn't changed at all. Its original virtues and values remain intact, despite the volatility of its march through the twentieth century and the triumphant battles waged against competitors. It's a company whose success has been built not on the manipulation of numbers but on a regard for the energy and creativity of people. Without the pride these people have felt—the harmony, the enthusiasm, and the determination to be ever better—the Shamrock story probably would have been significantly different.

Shamrock pride takes many forms, just as the business itself is multifaceted. There is pride in management, in the way the physical growth of the company has been orchestrated. There is pride of place, in the way the company has become part of every community it does business in or profits from. There is pride in its facilities, which have developed, evolved, and expanded over time. There is undeniable pride in its product, in all the categories of food and food-related items it both manufactures and distributes. Still, and from its earliest days, there is pride in the herd it has raised, in the prizewinning animals it has brought to the shows and fairs where cups and ribbons were awarded. Milt Sivesind expressed this pride in his unpublished reflections, written in the early 1980s.

MILT SIVESIND

It would be a great injustice to our company not to greatly emphasize the importance that Guernsey cattle have had in the success of this company. Mr. McClelland loved Guernseys. It seems to me that he sometimes held the whole of Shamrock together because of his love for the Guernseys. It seems to be the adhesive that gave him courage to keep on, regardless of the sometimes overwhelming odds. Mr. Mac had the qualities of a top athlete whose goal is to succeed over everyone else. It is a great lamentation that Mac and Mrs. Mac are not here today to see the results of their labors in family, friends, employee loyalty, and company goals realized. This independent, family-owned company is the only one that has succeeded to this degree in Arizona and Colorado, and I believe that if it had not been for the Guernseys, perhaps all this would not have happened.[1]

Where once the Shamrock herd provided all the milk sold under the familiar green label, Shamrock dairy products eventually came to include milk from scores of producers whose product flows daily into the plant's giant, cylindrical storage tanks. But Shamrock dairy cows still number among the company's treasured assets. The herd has grown, shrunk, and grown again, and the cows themselves have moved from one farm to another as the company's focus has shifted and as the Arizona population has grown so substantially that what was once farm country ultimately became suburbia.

At a management retreat in 1995, Shamrock began looking even farther down the road, beyond the turn of the century, to the year 2010. By that time, the attendees concluded, the company would be well established in four businesses.

NORMAN MCCLELLAND

We're in the milk business and the food-service business. We're already in the branded product business—Shamrock Farms Ice Cream brand, for example—and we've begun seeing a more branded product strategy by companies such as Knudsen on the West Coast, with their sour cream, buttermilk, and cottage cheese. So we're going to try to further our branded product business and also explore new opportunities to manufacture product that would be sold through our food-service divisions, such as we're already doing with vegetable oil products.

We talked about numerous other manufacturing opportunities that could be explored, items we would be producing on our own. For example, we could purchase a machine that would turn out plastic cutlery or even plastic trash containers. It is logical to assume that Shamrock could evolve into a number of different businesses, parallel businesses. Four seem plausible. Only time will tell; there's nothing finite here. We're looking at it one way this year, next year perhaps another way.

We're always reaching. We may not always grasp something, but the reaching itself is important; it's part of what we do. And, always, we do it for the same reason: to provide opportunities for people who are part of the organization, for the greater Shamrock family.[2]

During its years of growth, evolution, and change, Shamrock has been on the cutting edge of technology and process development. Despite having expanded dramatically, the company has managed to maintain family-style pride and dedication throughout its vast work force and, at the same time, keep its priorities in focus. "My father kept his first customers with just two things—quality and service," said Norman. "The company has kept and added customers with those same virtues—quality products and state-of-the-art service systems. And we will move forward with the same careful analysis of our customers' needs and how to fulfill them that has characterized us in the past. That's the service commitment everyone in Shamrock Foods Company shares."[3]

NORMAN McCLELLAND

> When we say Shamrock is a family company, we mean it in an extended sense. Every worker here is a member of the Shamrock family, with the opportunity to express ideas, contribute to the success of the company, and be recognized for his or her accomplishments. Without that family-style pride and loyalty, Shamrock wouldn't be where it is today. It's our greatest asset and our biggest priority.[4]

For Norman, family has always come first, whether it was this extended Shamrock family, which has burgeoned through the years, or his own family, which managed to flourish when it was pulled from its roots in Ireland and transplanted to the Arizona desert. As Mr. Mac became very much the assimilated American, the patriot prepared to defend the honor of his adopted homeland, Norman remained vividly aware of his Irish heritage and quick to acknowledge how much it had shaped his character and his approach to life: the Irish gift of gab, the embrace of sentiment and "Irish humor that sometimes cannot help seeming romantic, quirky, and quaint." Also, he insisted, "the Irish are very conscious of what's expected of them. I can remember a trip back to the family farm in Ireland when I was ten years old. It was a beautiful day and we were all out in the field harvesting oats. I was pounding a hammer on the sharpening stone and brought the whole proceedings to a halt when I broke the stone. My uncle was very angry and said, 'Now look what you've done—we won't be able to harvest. What will the neighbors think of us?' As my punishment, I was sent four miles to town on foot for a new stone."[5]

Frances McClelland always shared with her brother not only a respect for the family roots but a sense of obligation as well: "Being first-generation Americans, I think we feel a certain debt to this country, which has been so very generous to us and our whole family."[6] At the same time, both Frances and Norman have provided a generational bridge between the Old World upbringing of their immigrant parents and the New Age thinking of the generation poised to follow. With both feet planted firmly in the soil that nurtured them, they continued to look back on occasion to Ireland, where, as Norman described it, "the smells of the air are all of hay and of the sea, and one's total feeling is of being in a far place untouched by what we call progress.

"What the Irish traditionally bring with them to this country was best expressed, I think, in a poem by Stopford A. Brooke called 'The Earth and Man,' written more than a hundred years ago."[7]

A little sun, a little rain,
A soft wind blowing from the west,
And woods and fields are sweet again,
And warmth within the mountain's breast.

So simple is the earth we tread,
So quick with love and life her frame,
Ten thousand years have dawned and fled,
And still her magic is the same.

A little love, a little trust,
A soft impulse, a sudden dream,
And life as dry as desert dust
Is fresher than a mountain stream.

So simple is the heart of man,
So ready for new hope and joy;
Ten thousand years since it began
Have left it younger than a boy.[8]

For Shamrock, as for everyone in both its immediate and extended families, staying "younger than a boy" has meant never becoming complacent and always looking ahead—to new prospects and new opportunities. "What got Shamrock to where it is today is Norman P. McClelland, period," Dave Hall declared,[9] summing up his feelings about a man who, throughout their forty-year business relationship, remained a fierce exemplar of traditional Irish fortitude and all-American tenacity. Like his father before him, Norman has become a compelling role model for the many men and women who have worked with and for him. What surely will propel the company into the future is the energy, honesty, and extraordinary determination defined by his leadership and instilled in every member of the Shamrock team.

Norman put the ball in play; now, and in the years ahead, it will be up to the team to keep moving it forward.

Appendix

FLASH POINTS OF HISTORY

1891   W. T. McClelland, cofounder of Shamrock Dairy, is born to tenant farmers at Cloughenramer in County Down, Northern Ireland, on October 22.

1894   Sara Winifred Parker, future wife of W. T. McClelland, is born on a 35-acre farm at Ballykeel in County Down, Northern Ireland, on August 4.

1908   At age 17, W. T. McClelland is orphaned; with help from his sister and brother, he assumes management of the family farm.

1912   W. T. McClelland immigrates to America and settles in Arizona. For seven months he is a cowpuncher for the Triple C Ranch near Oracle.

1913   W. T. McClelland takes a new job, driving a delivery truck for Holstein Dairy, owned by Henry Peterson, in Tucson.

1916   W. T. McClelland returns to his Irish homeland for a brief visit.

1917   In January, W. T. is back in Arizona in Holstein Dairy's employ. In September he enlists in the U.S. Army and eventually serves overseas.

1919   W. T. McClelland earns an army discharge plus American citizenship and returns to Tucson to work for Holstein Dairy.

1920   W. T. quits his job and buys Modern Dairy, which he operates for a year. On December 27, he marries Winifred Parker, who has come from Ireland with her California-bound brother, William J. Parker.

1921   The McClellands sell Modern Dairy and travel to southern California, where they live for seven months before reacquiring Modern Dairy.

1922   Back in Tucson, the McClellands relocate the dairy and with 20 cows and a Model T Ford truck start their first milk delivery route. They call their joint venture Shamrock Dairy, named after Ireland's national emblem.

1923   The McClellands become parents of their first child, a daughter, Frances.

1925   A steady growth in business necessitates adding a second milk delivery route....In October, after a typhoid outbreak, the City Council of Tucson adopts a complete milk-pasteurization ordinance.

1926   Shamrock Dairy installs its first milk pasteurizer.

1927   The McClellands' second child, a son, Norman, is born.

1928   Mr. Mac adds a third milk route....On a trip to Wisconsin, he buys a cattle-car load of Guernsey cows.

1930   Shamrock's first rotary bottle filler and bottle washer are installed.

1933   William J. Parker leaves California to become a partner in Shamrock Dairy, which now has 10 employees and operates three retail routes and one wholesale route....Milking machines are in use in Arizona for the first time.

1934   Shamrock begins bottling milk in cream-top bottles and purchases Holstein Dairy from Henry Peterson.

1937   Yale Dairy is acquired, adding two more delivery routes to the existing nine, and tokens for purchasing milk products start being sold to Shamrock customers.

1938   Homogenized milk is introduced in Tucson.

1940   With eight retail and four wholesale routes, Shamrock builds a new office at the dairy.

1941   A new processing plant is built in Tucson. There are 35 employees and 15 vehicles.

1942   Because of wartime constraints, milk-delivery schedules are reduced to alternate days
        and daytimes only.

1943   In October, Mr. Mac and Clyde F. Rowe, a former University of Arizona professor, enter
        a partnership to operate Emerald Farms at Chandler, Arizona. The partnership will
        sustain until Mr. Rowe retires in 1967.

1945   Shamrock Dairy business has increased so much that 24 routes are needed.

1947   Waxed-paper cartons and Pur-Pak filling machines are installed in the dairy's
        processing plant.

1948   The McClellands' daughter, Frances, joins the Shamrock Dairy organization. She will
        eventually serve as secretary-treasurer on the board of directors.

1949   Shamrock Dairy establishes a scholarship fund so that each year one of Tucson's
        Amphitheater High School graduates will be awarded a $500 scholarship to attend the
        University of Arizona....A quality control laboratory is completed....The McClellands'
        son, Norman, joins the family business.

1950   Shamrock Dairy, which now serves 33 retail and 11 wholesale routes, builds a new
        garage, warehouse, and lunchroom....The company's first Employees' Retirement and
        Profit-Sharing Plan is instituted.

1951   Shamrock Dairy's first refrigerated truck is purchased.

1953   The Shamrock Milk Transport Company is formed; it is equipped with four tankers and four leased tractors....With refrigerated trucks now in use, electrical plug-in areas are built to handle a potentially all-refrigerated fleet....A hospitality room is included in the new office building erected at the Tucson plant. For the next 31 years— through films, exhibits, and demonstrations—it explains the milk-making process to schoolchildren and other visitors from around the world.

1954   In January, Shamrock Dairy Federal Credit Union is organized; in April, the Welfare Benefit Association is organized to help Shamrock families with special needs....In October, Shamrock Dairy of Phoenix is incorporated, and 10 acres of land fronting on Black Canyon Highway are purchased for $50,000 as a future building site....Mr. Mac becomes chairman as Norman assumes Shamrock's presidency.

1955   In January, Shamrock Hill Farm in Tucson is set up as a separate company....By summer, Shamrock's independent distributorship program is fully operational....In October, David B. Hall joins Shamrock, eventually becoming senior vice president....In November, the milk business of Cloverleaf Dairy in Bisbee, Arizona, is acquired.

1956   Shamrock Dairy of Phoenix builds its new plant for $318,855 and equips it completely for $255,000, including a liquid processing facility plus a culture room for the manufacture of sour cream, cottage cheese, and buttermilk.

1958   Shamrock acquires Jersey Farms Dairy of Yuma and purchases the Malin Lewis milk-distribution operation in the Yuma area.

1959   In May, Desert Gold Dairy of Casa Grande is acquired from Sam Parks, and Shamrock's product line is expanded to include ice cream products....In November, Purity Dairy of Douglas, Arizona, is acquired from August Patterson, and Purity dairy products are placed in the Shamrock distribution system....In December, Shamrock Guernsey Farm builds a new milking parlor, corrals, and a viewing area.

1960   Sunland Dairy in Yuma is purchased from Chad Cox, giving Shamrock entre'e into the ice cream manufacturing business once again.

1961   The dairy business in Coolidge, Arizona, is purchased from James Cooper....Shamrock's Tucson plant adds a large cold room with individual load-out areas, and the plant's conveyor system is redesigned to accommodate new stackers and casers.

1962   In late summer, New Modern Dairy becomes part of Shamrock after purchase from the Smith family....In the fall, Shamrock celebrates its 40th anniversary with open houses in Tucson, Phoenix, and Yuma.

1964   The first plastic containers, including 10-quart milk packages and doughnut-handled fruit drink containers, are added to the Shamrock product line....Prescott Farms Dairy of northern Arizona is acquired.

1965   In January, Shamrock buys the retail distribution of Sweet Milk Dairy in Phoenix....In May, Roosevelt Dairy of Mesa, Arizona, is acquired, and "filled milk" products are added to the Shamrock line—among them, Special M, Coffee Blend, White Satin, Whip Topping, and Special M Chocolate....In November, Shamrock Hill Farm moves to Cortaro Farms Road, in Tucson, with a new milking barn and the capability of milking 1,000 cows daily....A new milking barn is built at Emerald Farms, in Chandler, and the number of cows milked reaches 365.

1966   In January, Dora Brothers Distribution Company and its institutional foods operation are acquired, thereby providing Shamrock with membership in the Frozen Food Forum of America....In April, 20 acres of industrial development land are purchased on West Encanto Boulevard, near the Phoenix dairy operation, and earmarked for future expansion.

1967   In March, a milk route in Arizona's Kearny-Winkelman area is established when Shamrock buys Cow Palace Farms, Inc....In July, Robert E. Lee Institutional Foods is purchased, marking the beginning of Shamrock's frozen-foods distribution in Tucson, and Monte Carlo Dairy of Nogales, Arizona, is acquired from Simon Mastich....In October, Shamrock Dairy, Inc., Shamrock Milk Transport Company, and Shamrock Dairy of Phoenix are consolidated as Shamrock Foods Company.

1968   Mr. Mac dies of heart failure at age 76, leaving management of Shamrock in the hands of Norman and Frances McClelland and their uncle, Bill Parker....The W. T. and Winifred McClelland Scholarships are established for worthy upperclassmen or graduate students in the University of Arizona's College of Agriculture....Chubbuck Dairy in Miami, Arizona, is acquired, providing extended service for Shamrock in the Globe-Miami-Superior area....Shamrock Guernsey Farm lead the nation in milk production for herds of 125 or more.

1969   In February, Shamrock's transport division begins hauling fresh produce to northern California, Oregon, and Washington, and back-hauling frozen foods....In April, the house-to-house retail distribution of Phoenix's Foremost Dairy becomes part of Shamrock....In May, the new Phoenix garage is completed, and the ice cream division of Sweet Milk is acquired....In August, Quality Foods, a Tucson-based institutional house specializing in dry and canned groceries and related items is purchased from John Thibodeaux....Shamrock Guernsey Farms again leads the nation in milk production for herds of 125 or more.

1970   In April, Arizona Frozen Foods and its meat plant are acquired and merged with Shamrock Institutional Foods....In July, Shamrock purchases Sarival Farms in Phoenix from Bill Rasmussen and acquires a major interest in Inland Frosted Foods, Inc., of Denver....In October, Shamrock purchases Emerald Isle Investment Company....By the end of the year, Shamrock Foods Company becomes the second largest distributor of Guernsey products in the United States, and Neslekcim Fortune Daisy becomes the world's highest producing Guernsey cow: 27,990 pounds of milk in 305 days at the age of three years, eleven months.

243

1971   With the acquisition of the wholesale milk distribution of Meadow Gold products in Arizona and certain assets of Associated Dairy Products Company, Shamrock adds 13 delivery routes in Tucson and Phoenix....New offices, including space for data processing equipment, are completed in Phoenix.... The fleet now numbers 400 vehicles of all types....Shamrock is invited to join Master Dairies, a nationwide collective buying combine....W. T. McClelland is posthumously awarded a Certificate of Honor by the Dairy Shrine Club during the World Dairy Expo in Madison, Wisconsin....Norman McClelland joins the board of directors of the American Guernsey Cattle Club; he will serve on it nine years.

1972   Shamrock is cited in federal antitrust litigation; it takes 13 years for the issues to be resolved.

1973   National Commission Company of Colorado Springs is acquired from Harvey Klunder and ultimately becomes known as Inland National Foods.

1975   United Food Service is Shamrock's biggest Colorado acquisition; it is merged with Inland to form Inland-United Food Service.

1976   Stehman Distribution Company of Greeley, Colorado, is purchased, strengthening Shamrock's base in northern Colorado and eastern Wyoming....Also acquired is the Sid Schwartz Distributing Company, a supplier of meat products, groceries, and some produce.

1977   Winifred McClelland, Shamrock's cofounder, dies at age 83 after a long illness.

1978   Continental Food Service of Colorado is acquired.

1980   Shamrock buys the Berry-Losee Food Equipment Supply Company from the Berry brothers, Lowell and Kent.

1981   Shamrock is cited as a "Great Distributor Organization" by *Institutional Distribution* magazine, which devotes 13 articles in its June issue to the Shamrock "success story."

1982   The Arizona assets of the Romney Produce Company are absorbed by Shamrock, which now becomes the tenth largest food-service operation in the United States, serving Arizona and Colorado....In Phoenix, a new 2,300-square-foot tabletop and equipment showroom opens in the West Encanto Boulevard warehouse, and Arizona Lobsters and Seafood Company is acquired, adding Maine lobster to Shamrock's product line.

1983   The Chandler herd is moved to a new Shamrock Farms facility at Chandler Heights built for Jim Parker as a settlement of the Parker family's interest in Shamrock.... Shamrock's first mega-warehouse opens in Commerce City, Colorado, and the name Inland-United Food Service is changed to Shamrock Foods....In Phoenix, a blow-mold facility is installed in the dairy, enabling Shamrock to manufacture its own plastic containers....On July 13, credit union assets exceed $2 million for the first time.

1984   Norman's son, Kent, joins the management team in Denver, rising to division president and general manager before returning to Phoenix in 1992....With the acquisition of Frigid Products in Phoenix, Shamrock becomes capable of manufacturing all stick novelties, ice cream sandwiches, and sundae cups.

1985   Mile Hi Fruit & Vegetable Company merges its sales and delivery systems into Shamrock's Colorado foods division; Mile Hi Frozen Foods continues as a separate entity....Also in Denver, Restaurant Equipment and Design (REDCO) joins the Shamrock family, expanding tabletop business prospects dramatically....With Frigid Products comfortably under the Shamrock umbrella, the ice cream operation can finally be shifted from Yuma to Phoenix....Markon, a new produce buying cooperative, makes its first shipment to Shamrock and other constituent food service companies.

1986   Two new 50,000-gallon milk silo storage tanks are erected in front of the Phoenix milk plant; each is 64 feet tall and supported by pillars buried 25 feet underground.

1987   William J. Parker, a partner with his sister and brother-in-law since the early days of
        Shamrock Dairy, dies in Tucson at age 88....The acquisition of White Swan Foods and
        the food-service division of Fleming Foods' Arizona operation solidifies Shamrock's
        position as the number-one food-service company in the Southwest....Shamrock also
        becomes number one in sales volume for privately owned companies in Arizona,
        according to Arthur Andersen-compiled statistics based on 1986 revenues....Norman
        and Frances McClelland pledge $2.5 million toward construction of McClelland Hall at
        the Business College of the University of Arizona.

1988   Shamrock's first calves conceived by embryo transplantation are born.

1989   Shamrock builds a new dairy farm in Wickenburg, Arizona, to trade with Parker Dairy
        Farms for the Chandler Heights facility....In Denver, Booth Fisheries Distribution Center
        is acquired, providing entrée into the fresh seafood market in the five states served by
        Shamrock's Colorado operation....Jensen Foods of Brighton, Colorado, is purchased....
        With acquisition of the Piacere System, the Colorado beverage department now
        includes espresso and cappuccino coffee-making equipment.

1990   A new addition expands the size of the Commerce City, Colorado, warehouse from
        3,750,000 cubic feet to 9,000,250 cubic feet, providing a total of 270,000 square feet of
        storage space plus room for five new offices....Ace Poultry Company of Tucson is
        purchased, expanding Shamrock's chicken and egg service in southern Arizona....
        Shamrock Foods Company receives the "Most Admired Company" award from the
        Arizona 100 compilation and the Arizona Growth Award from the Arizona Chapter of
        the Association for Corporate Growth.

1991   In May, Norman McClelland is awarded an honorary doctor of laws degree during
        commencement exercises at the University of Arizona and is named Supplier of the Year
        (1990) by the Retail Grocers Association of Arizona....In September, the Tucson foods
        staff moves into a newly remodeled Foods Building.

1992   Kent McClelland becomes president and chief operating officer of Shamrock Foods, as Norman assumes the role of chairman and chief executive officer....Two more silo tanks are installed in front of the Phoenix plant, replacing older, smaller storage units; raw milk storage capacity is now close to 190,000 gallons.

1993   Shamrock Foods Company is listed among *Forbes* magazine's top 400 private companies in the United States for the first time.

1994   A new cooler at the food-service warehouse in Phoenix nearly doubles the refrigerated storage and dock capacity (from 31,000 square feet of storage and 9,000 square feet of dock space to 60,000 and 17,000 square feet, respectively)....Shamrock Premium Ice Cream debuts improved formulas, new flavors, and new packaging to match—and hopefully exceed—the competition....A new commodity barn is completed at Chandler Heights to handle farm growth.

1995   A new ammoniated refrigeration plant and a spiral freezer for hardening packaged ice cream become operational in Phoenix....The milk plant is expanded to increase pasteurizing and filling capacity by 50 percent....The Arizona Foods Division moves into 60,000 square feet of newly remodeled offices on West Encanto Boulevard....Shamrock is recognized as an outstanding company by The Newcomen Society of the United States, and Norman McClelland is the featured speaker at the Society dinner in Phoenix.

1996   Once again Shamrock is named a "Great Distributor Organization" by *Institutional Distribution* magazine....Sun Street Dairy closes its Phoenix Central Avenue plant, and Shamrock begins serving Carnation milk and ice cream customers....Shamrock buys ice cream inventory from Specialty Foods and is appointed distributor for Haagen Däzs ice cream products....A new, fully automated ASRS warehouse for Shamrock's Arizona Foods Division is being planned....The history of Shamrock is published in book form.

Acknowledgments

Compiling this history was a team effort on many levels. It could not have been done without the enthusiasm, cooperation, and participation of Norman, Frances, and Kent McClelland, and Dave Hall. Each of them willingly subjected themselves to long hours of being interviewed followed by equally long hours of reviewing and dissecting the finished text. Other members of the extended Shamrock family, both present and past, were inordinately generous and forthcoming, producing essays and participating in interviews that added measurably—in terms of anecdote and fact—to the history.

The author is particularly indebted to J. Morris Richards, who began assembling the Shamrock story in the early 1980s; to Carolyn Lagrand and Jann Browning, who were so responsive to long-distance calls for assistance and support; to Bruce Macomber, who created the index and put his editorial blue pencil to a much worked-over text; to Alfred Fariello, who faithfully transcribed hour upon hour of tape-recorded interviews; and, finally, to Curtiss and Anne Anderson, who passed along the assignment, saying, "This is a project that you should do."

Chapter Notes

1. Passing the Torch

1. Frances McClelland, interviewed in Phoenix by Anne Anderson and MK, October 1993.

2. Oliver Stallings, interviewed in Phoenix by Curtiss and Anne Anderson, April 1993.

3. Derrell Fairfield, interviewed in Phoenix by Curtiss and Anne Anderson, April 1993.

4. Ibid.

5. Oliver Stallings, interviewed in Phoenix by Curtiss and Anne Anderson, April 1993.

6. Clifford Knight, interviewed in Tucson by Frances McClelland, Norman McClelland, and Robert Whitehurst, August 1983.

7. Dr. Gary Stott, interviewed in Tucson by Lynda Morse, July 1983.

8. Norman McClelland, interviewed in Phoenix by MK, April 1994.

9. David Hall, interviewed in Phoenix by Mervyn Kaufman, April 1994.

10. Eloise Hayden, interviewed in Phoenix by Helen Coates, May 1983.

11. Norman McClelland, interviewed in Phoenix by MK, April 1994.

12. Frances McClelland, interviewed in Phoenix by Anne Anderson and MK, October 1993.

13. Oliver Stallings, interviewed in Phoenix by Curtiss and Anne Anderson, April 1993.

14. Norman McClelland, interviewed in Phoenix by Anne Anderson and MK, October 1993.

15. Ibid.

16, Ibid.

17. Bill Boyce, interviewed in Phoenix by David Hall and MK, April 1994.

18. John Underwood, interviewed in Phoenix by David Hall and MK, October 1993.

19. David Hall, interviewed in Phoenix by Helen Coates, March 1983.

20. Noman McClelland, interviewed in Phoenix by Anne Anderson and MK, October 1993.

21. David Hall, interviewed in Phoenix by MK, April 1994.

22. Norman McClelland, in essay drafted for unpublished company history compiled by J. Morris Richards, circa 1980.

23. Frances McClelland, interviewed in Phoenix by Anne Anderson and MK, October 1993.

2. Mr. and Mrs. Mac

1. Norman McClelland, in a speech delivered in Phoenix on the occasion of his sixty-fifth birthday, June 1992.

2. W. T. McClelland, interviewed in Tucson for unpublished company history compiled by J. Morris Richards, circa 1980.

3. Ibid.

4. William J. Parker, interviewed in Tucson by Frances McClelland, circa 1980.

5. Ibid.

6. Clifford Knight, interviewed in Tucson by Frances McClelland, Norman McClelland, and Robert Whitehurst, August 1983.

7. Frances McClelland, in a statement drafted for unpublished company history compiled by J. Morris Richards, March 1983.

8. Frances McClelland, interviewed in Phoenix by Anne Anderson and MK, October 1993.

9. Ibid.

10. From an interview in Tucson with William J. Parker, Frances McClelland, and Mrs. Earl Bates, circa 1980.

11. From an unpublished company history compiled by J. Morris Richards, circa 1980.

12. From an interview in Tucson with William J. Parker, Frances McClelland, and Mrs. Earl Bates, circa 1980.

13. Frances McClelland, interviewed in Phoenix by Anne Anderson and MK, October 1983.

3. Flip of a Coin

1. Frances McCelland, interviewed in Phoenix by Anne Anderson and MK, October 1993.

2. Frances McClelland, from a speech given in Phoenix on the occasion of Norman McClelland's sixty-fifth birthday, June 1992.

3. From Frances McClelland's unpublished recollections, March 1983.

4. Daniel Jones, interviewed in Tucson by Frances McClelland, circa 1980.

5. Ibid.

6. Lamar Sherman, interviewed in Tucson by Cliff Vance, circa 1980.

7. Norman McClelland, interviewed in Phoenix by Anne Anderson and MK, October 1993.

8. Frances McClelland, from a speech given in Phoenix on the occasion of Norman McClelland's

sixty-fifth birthday, June 1992.

9. Robert Gromko, interviewed in Phoenix by Anne Anderson and MK, October 1993.

10. Milton Sivesind, unpublished essay on pasteurization, circa 1983.

11. John Underwood, interviewed in Phoenix by David Hall and MK, October 1993.

12. Mrs. Buck Roberts, interviewed in Tucson by Frances McClelland, April 1984.

13. Ibid.

14. Frances McClelland, interviewed in Phoenix by MK, June 1994.

15. David Hall, interviewed in Phoenix by MK, June 1994.

16. Milton Sivesind, unpublished oral history drafted circa 1980.

17. Lavona Hawkins, interviewed in Tucson by Frances McClelland, March 1983.

18. William J. Parker, interviewed in Tucson by Frances McClelland, circa 1980.

19. Ibid.

20. Frances McClelland, interviewed in Phoenix by Anne Anderson and MK, October 1993.

21. Norman McClelland, interviewed in Phoenix by Anne Anderson and MK, October 1993.

22. Ibid.

23. Frances McClelland, interviewed in Phoenix by Anne Anderson and MK, October 1993.

24. John Underwood, interviewed in Phoenix by David Hall and MK, October 1993.

4. The Second Decade and Beyond

1. Frances McClelland, interviewed in Phoenix by Anne Anderson and MK, October 1993.

2. Ibid.

3. Ibid.

4. Frances McClelland, interviewed in Phoenix by MK, June 1994.

5. William J. Parker, interviewed in Tucson by Frances McClelland, circa 1984.

6. Milton Sivesind, in unpublished "History Information," August 1983.

7. Norman McClelland, in unpublished "History Information," August 1983.

8. Ralph Van Sant, interviewed in Tucson by William J. Parker and Frances McClelland, circa 1980.

9. Ibid.

10. Daniel Jones, interviewed in Tucson by Frances McClelland, circa 1980.

11. Frances McClelland, in unpublished recollections, circa 1980.

12. Ralph Van Sant, interviewed in Tucson by William J. Parker and Frances McClelland, circa 1980.

13. Ken Orchekowsky, in unpublished "History Information," August 1983.

14. Daniel Jones, interviewed in Tucson by Frances McClelland, circa 1980.

15. Ken Orchekowsky, in unpublished "History Information," August 1983.

16. Daniel Jones, interviewed in Tucson by Frances McClelland, circa 1980.

17. Catherine Rowe Lindbloom, interviewed in Phoenix by Frances McClelland, January 1984.

18. Ibid.

19. From *Shamrock News* 8 (fall 1975): 2.

20. Henry Reading, in unpublished "History Information," August 1983.

5. New Leadership, New Directions

1. Norman McClelland, in a letter to MK, October 1994.

2. John Underwood, interviewed in Phoenix by David Hall and MK, October 1993.

3. Milton Sivesind, in unpublished essay, "Development of Engineering, Building and Equipment for Plant Facilities—Post World War II Years for Shamrock," circa 1983.

4. Frances McClelland, interviewed in Phoenix by Anne Anderson and MK, October 1993.

5. Mrs. Buck Roberts, interviewed in Tucson by Frances McClelland, April 1984.

6. Frances McClelland, in unpublished recollections, March 1983.

7. Ibid.

8. Frances McClelland, interviewed in Phoenix by Anne Anderson and MK, October 1993.

9. Norman McClelland, in unpublished "Biographical Information," circa 1983.

10. Norman McClelland, interviewed by Anne Anderson and MK, October 1993.

11. Norman McClelland, in memorandum to MK, August 1995.

12. Norman McClelland, in unpublished "Biographical Information," circa 1983.

13. Norman McClelland, interviewed in Phoenix by Anne Anderson and MK, October 1993.

14. Milton Sivesind, in unpublished essay, "Quality," circa 1980.

15. Norman McClelland, in unpublished essay,"Shamrock History: Early Years and Building the Business," circa 1983.

16. Dick Oxnan, interviewed in Tucson by Cliff Vance, February 1983.

17. Norman McClelland, interviewed in Phoenix by Anne Anderson and MK, October 1993.

18. Norman McClelland, in unpublished essay, "Shamrock History: Early Years and Building the Business," circa 1983.

19. Ibid.

20. Johnny Torres, interviewed in Tucson by Ken Orchekowsky, circa 1980.

6. Acquisitions and Ice Cream

1. Norman McClelland, in unpublished essay, "Shamrock History: Early Years and Building the Business," circa 1980.

2. Helen Coates, self-interview in Phoenix, May 1983.

3. Ibid.

4. David Hall, in unpublished company history compiled by J. Morris Richards, circa 1980.

5. Ibid.

6. Norman McClelland, in unpublished "Shamrock History: Early Years and Building the Business," circa 1980.

7. Ibid.

8. David Hall, interviewed in Phoenix by Helen Coates, March 1983.

9. David Hall, in unpublished "History Information," March 1984.

10. Ibid.

11. Chad Cox, in unpublished essay, "Sunland Dairy," May 1983.

12. Joe Williams, in unpublished handwritten recollections, circa 1983.

13. Chad Cox, in unpublished essay, "Sunland Dairy," May 1983.

14. Milton Sivesind, in unpublished essay, "Yuma Ice Cream Plant," circa 1984.

15. Joe Williams, in unpublished handwritten recollections, circa 1983.

16. Milton Sivesind, in unpublished essay, "Yuma Ice Cream Plant," circa 1984.

17. Milton Sivesind, in unpublished "Shamrock History," circa 1983.

7. Following the Herd

1. From "Shamrock Golden Guernseys Among the Tops in the Nation," reprinted in *Shamrock News*, 27 (winter 1994): 20.

2. Ted Springer, unpublished self-interview, March 1983.

3. Norman McClelland, in *Shamrock News* 13 (summer 1980): 4.

4. Frances McClelland, interviewed inn Phoenix by MK, June 1994.

5. From "Chandler Heights New Farm Is Operating" by Jim Parker, *Shamrock News* 16 (spring 1983): unpaged.

6. Frances McClelland, interviewed in Phoenix by MK, June 1994.

7. From "It's the Latest" by Jim Parker, *Shamrock News* 22 (fall 1989): 16.

8. From "Meet Susie Upson" by Susie Upson, *Shamrock News* 14 (spring 1981): 6.

9. Ibid.

10. Ibid.

11. From "They're Here! Shamrock's own E.T.'s (Baby M's)" by Bob Whitehurst, *Shamrock News* 21 (spring 1988): 12.

12. Ibid.

13. Frances McClelland, interviewed in Phoenix by Anne Anderson and MK, October 1993.

14. From "Chandler Farms" by Charlotte Long, *Shamrock News* 27 (summer 1994): 46.

15. Norman McClelland, in unpublished "Shamrock History Comments," August 1995.

8. A Brand-New Business

1. David Hall, interviewed in Phoenix by MK, April 1994.

2. Ibid.

3. David Hall, in unpublished "History Information," March 1984.

4. Ibid.

5. Norman McClelland, in memorandum to MK, August 1995.

6. Norman McClelland, in unpublished essay, "Shamrock History: Early Years and Building the Business," circa 1980.

7. David Hall, in unpublished "History Information," March 1984.

8. Norman McClelland, in unpublished essay, "Shamrock History: Early Years and Building the Business," circa 1980.

9. David Hall, interviewed in Phoenix by MK, April 1994.

10. Harold Hornbeck, interviewed in Phoenix by Helen Coates, May 1983.

11. David Hall, in unpublished "History Information," March 1984.

12. Ibid.

13. Ibid.

14. Don Van Wormer, interviewed in Phoenix by MK, April 1994.

15. From "History," an unpublished report by Mrs. Edith Stallings, circa 1980.

16. From unpublished material supplied to company historian, J. Morris Richards, circa 1980.

17. Ted Springer, in unpublished self-interview, March 1983.

18. Frances McClelland, interviewed in Phoenix by MK, August 1995.

9. Colorado—From the Beginning

1. David Hall, in unpublished "History Information," March 1984.

2. Ibid.

3. David Hall, interviewed in Phoenix by MK, August 1995.

4. David Hall, interviewed in Phoenix by Helen Coates, March 1983.

5. David Hall, interviewed in Phoenix by MK, June 1994.

6. Ibid.

7. David Hall, in unpublished "History Information," March 1984.

8. Frances McClelland, interviewed in Phoenix by Anne Anderson and MK, October 1993.

9. Norman McClelland, interviewed in Phoenix by Anne Anderson and MK, October 1993.

10. Frances McClelland, interviewed in Phoenix by Anne Anderson and MK, October 1993.

11. Charles Andrews, interviewed in Phoenix by MK, April 1994.

12. Ibid.

13. Ibid.

14. Ibid.

15. Ibid.

16. Ibid.

17. Ibid.

18. Ibid.

19. Ibid.

20. Michael Mueller, interviewed in Commerce City, Colorado, by MK, September 1994.

21. David Hall, interviewed in Phoenix by MK, April 1994.

22. Michael Mueller, interviewed in Commerce City, Colorado, by MK, September 1994.

23. David Hall, interviewed in Phoenix by MK, April 1994.

24. Michael Mueller, interviewed in Commerce City, Colorado, by MK, September 1994.

10. Third-Generation Leadership

1. Norman McClelland, interviewed in Phoenix by Anne Anderson and MK, October 1993.

2. Kent McClelland, interviewed by phone by MK, March 1995.

3. Ibid.

4. Ibid.

5. Ibid.

6. Kent McClelland, interviewed in Phoenix by Anne Anderson and MK, October 1993.

7. Ibid.

8. Ibid.

9. From *Shamrock News* 19 (winter 1986): 4.

10. From *Shamrock News* 25 (winter 1992): 2.

11. Wheels of Change

1. From *Shamrock News* 25 (spring 1992): 31.

2. Carl Mrusek, unpublished self-interview, circa 1980.

3. Derrell Fairfield, interviewed in Phoenix by Curtiss and Anne Anderson, April 1993.

4. Ossie Koepp, interviewed in Phoenix by Ken Orchekowsky, circa 1980.

5. John Underwood, interviewed in Phoenix by Cliff Vance, June 1983.

6. Ibid.

7. John Harty, interviewed in Phoenix by Helen Coates, April 1983.

8. F. Phillips Giltner, interviewed in Phoenix by MK, April 1994.

9. Derrell Fairfield, interviewed in Phoenix by Bonnie Brown, April 1983.

10. Derrell Fairfield, interviewed in Phoenix by Curtiss and Anne Anderson, April 1993.

11. John Underwood, interviewed in Phoenix by Cliff Vance, June 1983.

12. Derrell Fairfield, interviewed in Phoenix by Bonnie Brown, April 1983.

13. Derrell Fairfield, in unpublished "History Information," September 1983.

14. Derrell Fairfield, interviewed in Phoenix by Bonnie Brown, April 1983.

15. Louis "Chubby" Frede, interviewed in Tucson by Ken Orchekowsky, circa 1980.

16. Derrell Fairfield, interviewed in Phoenix by Bonnie Brown, April 1983.

17. Norman McClelland, in unpublished essay, "Shamrock History: Early Years and Building the Business," circa 1980.

18. F. Phillips Giltner, interviewed in Phoenix by MK, April 1994.

19. David Hall, interviewed in Phoenix by MK, April 1994.

20. Derrell Fairfield, interviewed in Phoenix by Curtiss and Anne Anderson, April 1993.

21. Don Van Wormer, interviewed in Phoenix by MK, April 1994.

22. Ibid.

23. From *Shamrock News* 25 (spring 1992): 31.

24. Ibid.

25. Robert Gray, interviewed in Phoenix by Anne Anderson and MK, October 1993.

26. David Hall, interviewed in Phoenix by Anne Anderson and MK, October 1993.

27. Ibid.

28. Robert Gray, interviewed in Phoenix by Anne Anderson and MK, October 1994.

29. Ibid.

30. Robert Gromko, interviewed in Phoenix by MK, April 1994.

31. Ibid.

32. Robert Gray, interviewed in Phoenix by Anne Anderson and MK, October 1993.

33. David Hall, interviewed in Phoenix by Anne Anderson and MK, October 1993.

34. Ibid.

35. Kent McClelland, interviewed by phone by MK, December 1993.

36. Ibid.

12. Enjoying Success, Enduring Adversity

1. David Hall, interviewed in Phoenix by MK, August 1995.

2. From unpublished company history compiled by J. Morris Richards, circa 1983.

3. Derrell Fairfield, quoted in unpublished company history compiled by J. Morris Richards, circa 1983.

4. From *Institutional Distribution* 17 (June 1981); 59.

5. From *Institutional Distribution* 17 (June 1981): 61.

6. Norman McClelland, interviewed in Phoenix by Anne Anderson and MK, October 1993.

7. Ibid.

8. Norman McClelland, in memorandum to MK, August 1995.

9. From Norman McClelland statement to the court and to the press, January 1976.

10. Norman McClelland, in a letter to David L. White of Jennings, Strouss & Salmon, Phoenix, July 1994.

11. From Norman McClelland statement to the court and to the press, January 1976.

12. Ibid.

13. Norman McClelland statement to Shamrock employees during meetings held in Phoenix, May 11 and 12, 1987.

14. David L. White, in letter to Norman McClelland, July 1994.

15. Norman McClelland, in a letter to David L. White of Jennings, Strouss & Salmon, Phoenix, July 1994.

13. Mega-Warehousing

1. From *Shamrock News* 17 (summer 1983): 16-18.

2. Ibid.

3. From *Shamrock News* 23 (spring 1990): 6.

4. Larry Noble, interviewed in Commerce City, Colorado, by MK, September 1994.

5. David Hall, interviewed in Commerce City, Colorado, by MK, September 1994.

6. Larry Noble, interviewed in Commerce City, Colorado, by MK, September 1994.

7. Ibid.

8. Ibid.

9. Ibid.

10. Kent Mullison, interviewed in Commerce City, Colorado, by MK, September 1994.

11. Ibid.

12. Ibid.

13. Ibid.

14. Ibid.

15. Larry Noble, interviewed in Commerce City, Colorado, by MK, September 1994.

16. Ibid.

17. Kent McClelland, interviewed in Phoenix by MK, April 1994.

18. Robert Gray, interviewed in Phoenix by Anne Anderson and MK, October 1993.

19. Ibid.

20. Ibid.

21. Larry Yancy, interviewed in Phoenix by MK, June 1994.

22. Ibid.

23. Ibid.

24. Ibid.

25. Ibid.

26. Ibid.

27. Robert Gromko, interviewed in Phoenix by MK, April 1994.

28. Ibid.

29. Ibid.

30. Ibid.

31. Ibid.

32. Ibid.

33. Ibid.

34. Kent McClelland, interviewed by phone by MK, December 1993.

35. Ibid.

36. Michael Krueger, interviewed in Phoenix by MK, April 1994.

37. Ibid.

14. The Team Concept

1. Kent McClelland, interviewed in Phoenix by MK, June 1994.

2. Ibid.

3. Larry Yancy, interviewed in Phoenix by MK, June 1994.

4. Kent McClelland, interviewed in Phoenix by MK, June 1994.

5. Ibid.

6. Ibid.

7. Ibid.

8. Larry Yancy, interviewed in Phoenix by MK, June 1994.

9. Kent McClelland, interviewed in Phoenix by MK, June 1994.

10. Ibid.

11. Norman McClelland, interviewed by Anne Anderson and MK, October 1993.

12. Kent McClelland, interviewed in Phoenix by MK, June 1994.

13. Ibid.

14. Ibid.

15. Larry Yancy, interviewed in Phoenix by MK, June 1994.

16. Kent McClelland, interviewed in Phoenix by MK, June 1994.

17. Ibid.

18. Larry Yancy, interviewed in Phoenix by MK, June 1994.

19. John Ceraulo, interviewed in Phoenix by MK, June 1994.

20. Ibid.

21. Ibid.

22. Ibid.

23. Ibid.

24. Kent Mullison, interviewed in Commerce City, Colorado, by MK, September 1994.

25. Ibid.

26. John Maier, interviewed in Commerce City, Colorado, by MK, September 1994.

27. Ibid.

28. Robert Beake, interviewed in Commerce City, Colorado, by MK, September 1994.

29. Ibid.

30. Kent McClelland, interviewed in Phoenix by MK, June 1994.

15. Four Businesses

1. Milton Sivesind, in unpublished essay, "Dairies in Tucson That Sold Bottled Milk," April 1983.

2. Norman McClelland, interviewed in Phoenix by MK, August 1995.

3. Norman McClelland, quoted in "Shamrock Foods Company: In the Business of Delivering Quality and Service for 60 Years" (unpublished), 1983.

4. From "Shamrock Dairy: 60 Years Young" by Norman McClelland, *Shamrock News* 15 (fall 1982): 2.

5. Norman McClelland, in a speech given in Phoenix on the occasion of his sixty-fifth birthday, June 1992.

6. Frances McClelland, interviewed in Phoenix by MK, June 1994.

7. Norman McClelland, in a speech given in Phoenix on the occasion of his sixty-fifth birthday, June 1992.

8. From *A Treasury of Irish Poetry in the English Tongue*, edited by Stopford A. Brooke and T.W. Rolleston (New York: The Macmillan Company, 1923).

9. David Hall, in a letter to MK, July 1995.

Index